Financial Revival

A Lifestyle of Freedom

Financial *Revival*

A Lifestyle of *Freedom*

KRISTEN ECKSTEIN

Discover! BOOKS™
an Imprint of Imagine! Books™
High Point, North Carolina

Published by Discover! Books™
an Imprint of Imagine! Books™
PO Box 16268, High Point, NC 27261
contact@artsimagine.com

Imagine! Books™ is an enterprise of Imagine! Studios™
Visit us online at www.artsimagine.com

Copyright © 2010 Kristen Eckstein

Cover Design © 2010 Imagine! Studios™

All rights reserved. No part of this publication may be reproduced or transmitted in any form or by any means, including informational storage and retrieval systems, without permission in writing from the copyright holder, except for brief quotations in a review.

This book's content is for informational purposes only and is not intended to replace professional financial advice.

All scripture quotations, unless otherwise indicated, are taken from the Holy Bible, New International Version®, NIV®. Copyright ©1973, 1978, 1984 by Biblica, Inc.™ Used by permission of Zondervan. All rights reserved worldwide. www.zondervan.com

Scripture quotations (marked ESV) are from The Holy Bible, English Standard Version® (ESV®), copyright © 2001 by Crossway, a publishing ministry of Good News Publishers. Used by permission. All rights reserved.

Scripture quotations marked "NKJV™" are taken from the New King James Version®. Copyright © 1982 by Thomas Nelson, Inc. Used by permission. All rights reserved.

ISBN 13: 978-0-9767913-6-2
Library of Congress Control Number: 2010927748
First Discover! Books™ printing, April 2010

Table of Contents

Foreword 11
Introduction 17
Chapter 1: Your Identity 21
Chapter 2: God's Identity 33
Chapter 3: Limiting God 43
Chapter 4: Poverty 53
Chapter 5: Stewardship 71
Chapter 6: Obedience 83
Chapter 7: Prosperity 99
Chapter 8: Generosity 113
Chapter 9: God's Economy 121
Chapter 10: The Tithe 139
Chapter 11: The Offering 153
Chapter 12: Declaration 165
Appendix 175
About the Author 181

"Each one must do just as he has purposed in his heart, not grudgingly or under compulsion, for *God loves a cheerful giver.*"

2 Corinthians 9:7

This Book is Dedicated:

To my husband, whose never-ending support enables me not only to write, but to live daily what I write.

To my earthly parents, who taught me the meaning of giving and how to be a true daughter of God.

To Forward Financial Group and Dave Knopp, who first opened my eyes to why we give, and how to tap into God's Kingdom.

To my pastor, Whitman Toland, who continually teaches us the values of living in God's Kingdom, despite the opposition.

To my Abba Father, Jehovah Jireh, the reason why I write. The words in this book belong to Him. I am but His tool to put them on paper.

Foreword

By Pastor Whitman Toland, C3 Greensboro

The world's view of prosperity is focused on the finances in your bank. God's view of prosperity is that it will touch your finances, but it's more of a mindset. It's a way we view—lenses we look through. Proverbs 22:9 says, "He who has a generous eye will be blessed" (NKJV). It's how we should view life—with a Kingdom mindset of prosperity.

In our humanity, any kingdom principle can be manipulated, used, or directed to serve "self." This is what we know of as "Prosperity Doctrine" today. It creates a mindset of, "If I do this… then God will do this…" or "If I give, God's going to prosper me so I can get what I want." The doctrine in and of itself can leave out God's intention for prosperity—His real purpose for it.

God's intention is that prosperity doesn't just stop with us. I am not the end goal, but rather I become a conduit for resources to flow through. I'm not a pond or container for prosperity to flow to, I'm a conduit for resources, including money, knowledge, anointing, peace, etc. A pond that doesn't have an outlet becomes stagnant, as does prosperity if not handled God's way.

Our mindset should be, "God has blessed me because..." We are blessed to be a blessing. When we are walking in the blessing God has for us, we will encounter what I call the perfect storm. For example, when our church moved to a new building, Hell raged, like a four-cylinder engine to trying to drive an 18-wheeler... How we operated for 10 years is changing. We know where we're going, but not how we're going to do it. We need to act 5-star, with excellence. We can't reach the way we need to—make a difference in our city—without being as excellent as God has called us to be. And that level of excellence requires finances.

> **Revival Tip:** *We are blessed to be a blessing.*

God doesn't have to tell us each week to tithe. We already know God's heart and intention. We don't need to pray about it. Matthew 4:4 says, "It is written, 'Man shall not live by bread alone, but by every word that proceeds from the mouth of God.'" In the area of our giving, God always nudges and speaks to people concerning how currency flows. Jesus doesn't walk in with a check drawn on someone else's bank account, He gives us an opportunity to give. He speaks, gives us the chance to be a blessing and sow into His Kingdom. He is looking for people He can flow through.

We should be learning to live in relationship with the Lord so we know his voice. "My sheep hear My voice, and

I know them, and they follow Me" (John 10:27). We love to hear the voice of God when it touches everything except money. Where our heart is, our finances are. Proverbs 3:5 says, "Trust in the Lord with all your heart." He said ***all***. There's a correlation between a demonstration of our trust and how we respond to the Lord's leading in giving. Giving is a trust issue, not a money issue. Giving is a response in obedience.

At the end of the day, giving is directly related to our love for the Lord versus our love for money. Is our security in the Lord or our money? The Lord will ask us to do things as a demonstration and reminder that our hope is in Him.

Over the last 10 years, we as a church have given over a half-million dollars to ministries and individuals in response to God's leading. By sowing into other churches, ministries, and people, we've held really loosely to our finances because they're actually God's anyway. It puts us in a position of having to believe God. We can't trust in our sowing—but we can trust God.

> **Revival Tip:** *We have to learn how to not quit when it looks bleak.*

Now we're in a position where we're believing that as sowing produces a harvest, we are declaring and we know our harvest as a church for the purposes we've been given will continue seed for the future. Obedience creates confidence that when we do what God asks us to do, it releases Him to do what only *He* can do. God is not quick to forget the things we have done for Him.

We get so anxious learning to wait for that harvest. We have had to learn how to not quit when it looks bleak. Sometimes you have to freakin' stand! We've been hit with everything possible and the devil will say, "Where is God in that?" But God is saying, "Are you going to love me when..." By building a proper relationship with our money where we don't give to get, our faith grows and we can stand on what God has promised.

> *Revival* Tip — ***Obedience creates confidence.***

It's not the amount—$100 or $1,000. It's about what God is saying. If I'm giving $1,000 and the Lord only asked for $100, it could hurt. He never asked for that, and then my kids need x-rays. If I'd given what the Lord said—$100, as He reminds me, I would have had the $900 for those x-rays and medical bills. Sometimes when God asks us to obey, we may hear a lower amount than we're able, which may be God working on a pride issue and also may be God providing for a future need He knows we are going to have. It helps us to see where our heart really is so we don't question—we just do it—no matter the amount.

What Kristen does in this book is take us from our personal relationship with God to growing in our identity all the way through being in a position to bless others as God has asked us to. Kristen does a brilliant job of walking us through the process because giving and our heart posture and our relationship with God are all so intertwined. In this book, Kristen defines how building the foundation of our relationship is the end goal instead of giving itself—how it is a byproduct of our relationship with God. It's not the mechanics or law of writing a check. This book lays out foundationally first things first, then grows as your faith grows to allow God to increase every aspect of your life.

Introduction

As I sat down to write this book, I asked myself the question I know will come from others. What qualifies me to write about this topic? I am not a financial planner. I have not made large investments in the stock market, real estate, or other classic areas of financial investment. I have not even taken a finance class.

As I pondered these questions and asked God why He put it on my heart to write about this topic in the first place, I heard clearly two things:

1. **We are living it.** This lifestyle, this act of daily walking in God's Kingdom in our finances, sowing and reaping. My family is actively taking part and seeing the hand of God at work. By living it, I am able to take what we have learned and put the message in an understandable format for the everyday person. It is not theology. It is a way of life that I personally believe God intends every one of His sons and daughters to follow.

2. **If God can use Moses, He can use me.** All I have asked is to be a vessel that can make

a difference in someone else's world. My husband and I have had the opportunity to speak into the lives of family and friends and see their situations transform before our very eyes. Moses couldn't even talk clearly, yet God wanted Him to lead the Israelites. If God has a message to deliver, what better way than to choose someone who has no experience so that when people do see real results in their lives, He gets all the glory?

As you read the words in this book, take them as from one who is living this life every day. Not someone who has appointed themselves a "financial" or "theological" expert, but someone just like you who deals with life day to day. I aim to make the language of this book clear, easy to understand, and above all in-line with God's word.

> **Revival Tip:** *If God could use Moses, He can use you.*

Some things may require prayer and revelation to sink deep enough in your heart where you know them to be true. Other things will make sense quickly. And still other points may be made that rub you the wrong way. You may not have been taught about God's financial Kingdom. Your church may not teach about tithing and giving. But the word of God teaches about tithing, giving, and your finances. So now it is time for you to learn what God is saying about you and your money. Your real purpose is about to begin!

"And you will be called priests of the Lord, you will be named ministers of our God. You will feed on the wealth of nations, and in their riches you will boast."

Isaiah 61:6

Chapter 1

Your Identity

Before you can establish anything else in your life, you must define your identity. This is not just "who you are" or "what you want to be when you grow up." It is not about "finding yourself." Rather, it is identifying who you are meant to be as God sees you. You, a special individual human being unlike any other on the earth. You, with all your faults and all your successes. You, above all, through God's eyes: a special creation meant to reflect His love to the world.

If you do not already believe all of these things about yourself, or all you can see are your faults and failures (often as defined by others or your circumstances), do not despair! By the end of this chapter, you will have a solid foundation of what God says about you. And who God says you are is what matters most.

> *Revival* Tip | **Who God says you are is what matters most.**

You Were a Cursed Creation

In the beginning, Adam and Eve were given a choice to obey or disobey God regarding the tree of the knowledge of good and evil. God warned them, as any good parent would, that if they disobeyed they would suffer serious consequences. They both disobeyed and as a result, God's perfect creation became cursed.

Whether you believe in the account of Genesis as true history or not, you cannot deny the evidence of a fallen world. A world filled with turmoil, grief, wars, hunger, poverty, and all the other bad things some people feel God "lets happen." The Bible is clear that these were not God's original intentions for mankind.

God followed through with His promised consequence, just as any good parent would. To not do so would make God a liar and untrustworthy. The promised consequence on the man was that he would have to work harder for what he needs and he would struggle with a fear of failure. The curse on the woman was pain in childbirth, and the desire to be head over her husband yet become frustrated when he is indecisive and doesn't respect her. They were also both cursed with spiritual and physical death (Genesis Chapter 3).

Because of this curse, God gave the law to the Israelites in the Old Testament as a foundation to live healthy, righteous lives. In Galatians 3:10 we see that God pronounced a curse on everyone who did not observe the law. *All who rely on observing the law are under a curse, for it is written: "Cursed is everyone who does not continue to do everything written in the*

Book of the Law." Adam's curse led to the law, which led to a curse on those who did not follow it.

As children of God, we did indeed live under the "curse of the law." *Christ redeemed us from the curse of the law by becoming a curse for us, for it is written: "Cursed is everyone who is hung on a tree"* (Galatians 3:13). This verse not only identifies that we lived under the curse, but it states right away that we do not need to live under this curse any longer. We have been *redeemed*, it says, from the curse Adam and Eve brought on the world. And the curse does not just apply to sickness, disease, injury, hunger, grief, and other major world disasters. It also applies to the finances in your daily life.

> **Revival Tip** — We do not need to live under the curse.

You Are a Son or Daughter

Isaiah 61:6, the beginning of which was quoted by Jesus in the temple in Luke 4, says, *And you will be called priests of the Lord, you will be named ministers of our God. You will feed on the wealth of nations, and in their riches you will boast.* This verse is defining your identity as a "priest of the Lord" or "minister." This does not mean you need to go to seminary and become a pastor, but rather that you, as a child of God having accepted Jesus' sacrifice and Him as your Savior, are a *carrier* of God's presence. Merriam-Webster lists one definition of a minister as an "agent," that is, "one who is authorized to act for or in the place of another." Because you are a minister of God, He has given you the means to accomplish what He wants you to accomplish in this world, including the ability to obtain and use finances. You have been given authority to come to God with your requests and carry out His will on the earth through your finances.

> **Revival Tip:** *You have been given authority to come to God with your requests.*

In addition to being ministers and priests, with that level of authority, Jesus paid the price for us to become sons and daughters with every inheritance and right that comes along with that title. Galatians 4:4–7 says, *But when the time had fully come, God sent his Son, born of a woman, born under law, ⁵to redeem those under law, that we might receive the full rights of sons. ⁶Because you are sons, God sent the Spirit of his Son into our hearts, the Spirit who calls out, "Abba, Father." ⁷So you are no longer a slave, but a son; and since you are a son, God has made you also an heir.*

Some may say that verse is describing our inheritance of heaven when we die (or are raptured). However, I believe that God wants to be our father *now*. And if He wants to be our father now, how does that withhold His hand of blessing? What father, in his right mind, would deny his child food when asked? Or water? Or the basic necessities of life? *Which of you, if his son asks for bread, will give him a stone?* (Matthew 7:9) And how many more parents do you know who want so much more for their children—more than they ever had themselves? What parent denies their children the ability to learn, grow, and anything that may take them to their desired future?

So if God is your Abba Father, who is to say He doesn't want the same as a good earthly father for you? Your identity is not only found in your earthly parents, but in God and His desires for your life. And He wants to give you a full inheritance—access to His Kingdom—even while you are still remaining on this earth. *If you, then, though you are evil, know how to give good gifts to your children, how much more will your Father in Heaven give good gifts to those who ask Him!* (Matthew 7:11)

You Are an Influencer

If you build your life on what you are not (a failure, not favored, an everyday run-of-the-mill worker of a daily grind job with no prospects) then you will never find out what you are. God desires you to discover who you truly are—in His eyes.

You may not see yourself as anything very special. But God sees you as the most important special creation He has ever made. Why else would He have sent the one He loved more than anything—His son—to redeem you?

What God desires most is for you to identify yourself to Him—through His eyes. When you see yourself as God sees you, you start walking into what He has for you. And believe me, what He has for you is often a lot greater than you can imagine. It can be scary at times, but He will give you what you need and put others in your path to help you reach your destiny. In Chapter 3, I will discuss more of what hinders people from receiving what God desires to give them. But for now, you need to know and understand that you are a vehicle. You are the path for God to reach your family, friends, neighbors, and ultimately your world. You are an influencer.

> **Revival Tip:** *It is an enlightening and scary experience to recognize what God has for you.*

You Are Who God Says You Are

Your purpose is not to continue in the ways you are going now, but to grab hold of the revelation of what God is saying about you and apply it to your daily life. For me, it was a physical exercise of asking God what He was saying about me. During a time of prayer, reading His Word, and worship, I asked God to tell me what He thought about me. I then took the thoughts that began flooding into my head and wrote them down. These are not just affirmations; they are a lot more powerful. They carry the weight of the ultimate power in the universe (and that's *not* science fiction).

I know these words were from my Abba Father, because I didn't see some of them manifest in my life yet and I never would have said some of them about myself. However, as time has gone on, I have seen the things God told me in that exercise of who I am come to fruition. It is an enlightening and scary experience to recognize what God has for you, who He says you are, and to begin to believe it. But it is part of the most amazing adventure you could ever begin.

Who God says you are is not always how you are currently living. Even if you are not blatantly disobeying God, or even if you try your best to do the right thing, He has something bigger and better to say about you. Try that exercise yourself. Put on some worship music, get in tune with God, and ask Him what He is saying about you and your life. Even if it doesn't make any sense, write it down. Write what you are feeling, impressions on your spirit.

Do not be discouraged if nothing comes right away. You need to put aside your personal feelings and desires and be open to what God says about you. And as you do the exercise, remember that your past does *not* determine your future! Don't worry—it will start to flow. Once you have the revelation of who you are and what you are called to do, stick it up where you will see it often (my list is my desktop wallpaper on my computer).

> *Revival Tip: **Your past does not determine your future!***

Once you get your revelation about who you are from God and start speaking it over your life daily, keep tabs on how you are doing. Are you reacting to something in the way God wants you to? The way He has said you are? Refer back to your list of things God has said about you. If you wrote down that you are a patient, caring person, yet you find yourself screaming at something that didn't go your way or someone who didn't do what you wanted them to the first time, maybe you need to reevaluate and see how you could handle that situation differently.

> **Revival Tip:** *Who does God say you are?*

Don't change your list. You will grow into the person God says you are, even if it isn't accurate right now. Always keep the light on in your life and know where you are headed. The enemy loves the little dark corners in our hearts, so the more often you evaluate yourself and ask to be forgiven (from God and people you may have hurt), the closer you will come to that list of identifiers God has given you.

You Are a Possessor of Finances

I know I have not covered anything financial yet. There is a purpose to this strategy. Until you define who you are in God's eyes, and realize who exactly God is, you will not be able to apply anything to your finances. You will not understand why God asks certain things of you.

Until you have absolute faith in who God says He is (covered in the next chapter), you may not be willing to take a couple you've never met out to lunch after church, or give a check to someone who is struggling, or do anything else God may be asking you to do with your money. You may want to, but you will not see how God is going to provide for your needs if you give away some of your limited funds.

Now that you have a clear understanding of who God says you are—a beloved son or daughter He desires to bless—let's take a closer look at who God says He is and why He must be an integral part of your financial future. You might be in for a surprise.

"'But what about you? ... Who do you say I am?'"

Matthew 16:15

Chapter 2

God's Identity

Let me say right off the bat that your perception of God's identity may not be totally accurate. Perhaps you see Him as an entity you cannot reach (ambiguous God). Maybe you view Him as the one to run to in times of trouble, who will bail you out of the circumstance you find yourself in (rescue God). Maybe you feel if you're giving money to the church, no matter the amount, He should be obligated to answer any request you may have (vending machine God).

There are also two other extreme views. Some believe God is an ogre ready to dispatch torturous punishment on anyone who would disobey Him (vengeance God). Others believe He is so kind and gentle that regardless of what you do you should not feel guilty or suffer because He would never allow someone to hurt or feel shame or guilt (wishy-washy God).

The truth is, none of these are correct. He is too vast for us to completely understand every aspect of His existence. You may have a lot of information about God (He saves, He lives in Heaven, He sent Jesus, etc.), but just because you have information does not mean you have a *revelation* of God's true identity. Only God Himself can provide you with a revelation of who He is. And hopefully this chapter will help.

He Is Revealer

We see a clear example of defining God's identity in Matthew 16:15–17, *"But what about you?" he asked. "Who do you say I am?"* ¹⁶*Simon Peter answered, "You are the Christ, the Son of the living God."* ¹⁷*Jesus replied, "Blessed are you, Simon son of Jonah, for this was not revealed to you by man, but by my Father in heaven."* When something is revealed to you by the Father, it is a revelation. A revelation is often characterized as an "a-ha moment," when something clicks deep inside your spirit and you just *know* it to be true.

> **Revival Tip:** *A revelation is like an "a-ha moment."*

You may have a lot of information and know a lot of facts about the Bible or religion in your mind, but unless you know in your spirit, I mean really *know*, you have not gotten a revelation. Many times, revelation is spoken over people's lives in a prophetic meeting, or when someone tells you something only God would know about you. Whenever you get a revelation, hang on to it. Write it down. Do not forget it. Once you have received a revelation, no one can take it away from you unless you let them.

Chapter 2: God's Identity

You will need this revelation to get you through trials. When hell rages, information won't get you anything. But, the gates of hell cannot prevail against who God really *is*. So now is the time to ask yourself, "Who is God?" Not "Who is God to me?" But, "Who is God Himself? What is His unique identity?"

> *Revival* Tip — *No one can take your revelation away from you unless you let them.*

He Is Jehovah Jireh

God has many names throughout the Bible. However, to me, one has stood out among all the others and it is especially important in relationship with your finances: *Jehovah Jireh*, which translated from Hebrew is *My Provider* or *God provides*. *And Abraham calleth the name of that place "Jehovah-Jireh," because it is said this day in the mount, "Jehovah doth provide"* (Genesis 22:14, YLT).

You may be in a pit of debt right now, but hold on to God's promise that He is Jehovah Jireh, your provider, and that you can make it out. You can't build your life on hope. Hope is good to get you through the rough times, but if all you ever do is hope, you will be left helpless. Instead of merely hoping things will change, make a clear decision to recognize God as your provider. Not just your pastor's provider, or your friend's provider, but *your* provider.

God is an unlimited source. By declaring Him as your source, you are able to tap into that limitless vast supply of Heaven.

He Is Giver

God is the ultimate giver. He has held nothing back from us. Not only did He create and give humans the entire earth to rule and subdue (Genesis 1), but He gave His only Son. John 3:16 says, *For God so loved the world that he gave his one and only Son, that whoever believes in him shall not perish but have eternal life.* God gave. He loved you so much, He gave. He gave you everything. Whatever your earlier perceptions of Him are, God is not a taker. He's the giver of life!

> **Revival Tip:** *God modeled His Kingdom by giving first.*

He modeled His Kingdom by giving *first*. He didn't wait for us to give anything to Him before He gave us everything. This is obvious in Genesis Chapters 1 and 2 when He created and gave Adam and Eve the entire earth. If He cared enough about humans to give them dominion over the whole earth, who are we to limit what He wants to give us?

The entire world belonged to God, and He chose to give it to us. So why do we often think He only wants to take something from us? Or that He must not want to give anything to us if we don't always get what we want when we want it?

Just as a good father won't spoil his children, because it is not to their benefit for them to always have what they want, God does not spoil His children. He will, however, give all we ask if it is in accordance with His will. And His will is for us to prosper beyond only taking care of our own needs. I will discuss this more in-depth later.

God Is Initiator

God's nature is to make the first move. He didn't wait around for humans to fix the world. He sent Jesus to do the job that man could not. Human nature waits to see how "I feel" before responding. It is always human nature to consider our personal concerns first in any decision. But God would rather we consider His concerns first.

How many times have you seen someone at the grocery store counting out pennies, then not having enough money for their groceries? Did you ever feel the nudge to buy the groceries for them? What about when you heard about someone in your church or community who was struggling? What held you back from helping them? Have you ever felt the nudge to take strangers out to eat after meeting them for the first time—your treat? What holds you back from following these nudges?

Maybe what has held you back are your own selfish desires. This may sound unfeeling, but it can be true. There have been times when I have spent money on something frivolous, when it would have been better spent elsewhere. I have often heard individuals complain that they can't pay their bills, yet see them posting online almost daily that they are going out to eat at nice restaurants, or the latest flavor from Starbucks they tried. The act of putting wants ahead of needs, I think we can all agree, is irresponsible, which is a form of selfishness that we are all guilty of. The key is to learn to be responsible with what God has entrusted to you and recognize when you are allowing selfishness to reign.

God's nature is not to spoil His children and create selfish brats. His nature is to honor responsibility. If you are not already responsible for what you have been given, what makes you think He can trust you with more? He is not going to yell at you to take someone out to lunch. He is not going to audibly announce over the grocery store intercom to buy someone's groceries. He uses "nudges"—that still, small voice—to guide you in the direction He wants you to go. If you have trouble feeling those nudges, your own voice is probably too loud. Our own selfish desires will drown out a God-given nudge.

> *Revival* Tip — **God's nature is to honor responsibility.**

A God-given nudge is like a whisper in your spirit. It is not a lightning bolt from heaven. God communicates to the deepest part of us first. He gets our attention by communicating with our spirits, the part of us that is most like Him. His Spirit can tell you what the right decision is by speaking directly to your spirit.

It is best described as a "whisper" because you can't hear it. In order to hear this whisper, you need to actually be still. You can hear it while God's word is preached, reading the Bible, or just listening when you need to make a decision or need assurance that you're heading in the right direction. In our frenzied, over-stimulated culture, the tendency is for us to hurry too much to listen. *Be still, and know that I am God* (Psalm 46:10).

> **Revival Tip:** *You are here to fulfill a greater purpose.*

Often, when I feel the nudge to treat a stranger to lunch, it is when I do not want to do anything on a Sunday afternoon but go home and relax. And I enjoy going out to eat, so this is highly unusual. But every time my husband and I have followed that nudge, God has created an amazing divine connection. Many times, that connection was an answer to a prayer we had temporarily given up on. Sometimes it has been a connection to someone we could bless above and beyond a simple lunch. Every time it has been amazing, and the more we act on the nudges, the more we recognize the next one when it comes.

God may not ask you to take someone out to lunch every Sunday. He may not ask you to do that at all. But He *is* asking you to do something. You were not put on this earth to take up space and live your daily life all alone. You are here to fulfill a greater purpose.

When we choose to honor God, follow His commands, and act in obedience even when it hurts, we will be blessed beyond measure. See Chapter 6 on Obedience for more detail.

With God, the rule is never "every action creates an equal and opposite reaction." The reaction He gives us when we follow His desires for our lives is always greater than what we do in obedience to Him. He only asks us for a little and in return He blesses us with much. By not taking that first step into understanding His nature, that He desires to bless us in order to be a blessing for others, we will never take the first step into walking in all God has for us—our real purpose and future.

> "Where there is no vision, the people perish."
>
> Proverbs 29:18

Chapter 3

Limiting God

Oftentimes, we do not see results in our world because we are limiting God. Whether you realize it or not, there are many factors at work that limit how God can move in your life. Some of these factors are under your direct control and should be changeable. Others are changeable only by unwavering faith as they are completely in God's control.

With Job "Security"

A job is designed to keep you coming back for more. Think about it. You go to work, you earn a paycheck. Why do you go back to work? To earn another paycheck. Believe it or not, a job does not create security. Especially in times of financial collapse, many people have realized they cannot put their trust in their jobs.

There is no guarantee that you will go home from work tomorrow still employed. Yet some employers and society tend to encourage us to purchase large things for our own consumption like houses, expensive cars, and other things that keep us in debt. Not just in debt to the creditors, but in debt to our jobs. Now you have to go back to work so that you can pay that credit card bill, that car payment, and the mortgage that is barely squeezing into your budget. Often, a job actually creates insecurity because you begin to worry if your next paycheck is going to be enough to cover your bills for the next term.

> **Revival Tip:** *A job doesn't give you power to be successful.*

A job doesn't give you power to be successful, even though some people think it does. If you have faith in your supervisor or job to make you successful, your faith is misplaced. You may think your job gives you financial success as you obtain raises, bonuses, promotions, or even simply remain employed, but the fact is your job is a training tool society uses to make you think that is the definition of "success." Using this definition, those in power over you have the ability to directly control how much success you have, and they can change the direction of it at their discretion. As a result, your faith naturally begins to be placed in your supervisors, employer, and job. The more faith you put in your job or employer, the more insecure you will become. In order to truly be successful by God's standards, you need to understand how He defines success.

God's idea of success is not just having a job that helps pad your life with creature comforts like a latte and bagel every morning. His definition of financial success is having enough money to change the world. And that is much more than any job can give you. He wants you to be successful in order to bless others and show them how they can do the same thing. Ephesians 4:28 says, *He who has been stealing must steal no longer, but must work, doing something useful with his own hands, that he may have something to share with those in need.* Clearly we are to make a living, but beyond that we are to use what we earn to help others.

You can take it a step further and define your success by how much you are able to give away, not how much is in your next paycheck. Thinking of it in that way will change your mindset away from your own selfish desires of how much money you take home and toward what God is telling you to do for others. For instance, in our business I have started to measure how successful we are in a given month by how much we give in tithe to our church and offerings to other ministries. I rarely look at the gross revenue our company brings in, but rather at how much we are able to share.

By working to give instead of to make a living, we are helping to define success according to God's standards. Above all, work so that you have something to share, not just to fill your own pockets.

By Lacking Vision

Another way we limit God is by taking what we see at face value. God's will is not automatic or easy. He's more concerned about building character than your comfort. Many times what we see with our natural eyes in our circumstances is not what God sees for us.

You may have heard the saying that some people see crisis where others see opportunity. This is very true. If you don't see the opportunity for God to work through your crisis, all you will see is the crisis itself.

> **Revival Tip:** *Some people see crisis. God sees opportunity.*

I have a friend who lived in an ongoing crisis for years. She had a job that paid well, but her boss was condescending and often did things she felt were ethically and morally wrong. Every time I tried to share with her what I saw as an outsider and how she could use the crisis as an opportunity to start the business that was in her heart, she would understand what I was saying. However, she was not willing to take that chance, that first step of faith, because she could not see how God would provide.

If you don't see it, God can't do it. You may not be able to see it with your natural eyes, but we're talking about seeing with your heart. Psalm 119:11 says, *I have hidden your word in my heart that I might not sin against you.* Sinning against God is not always defined as blatantly breaking His laws. Sometimes we sin by simply not believing what He says.

Vision is always unfolding. It grows and changes, just as you grow and change. When you begin stepping into the vision God has given you for your life, you will see more of that vision and a broader expanse of your Promised Land.

Do not limit God by limiting your potential to only what you see naturally. Philippians 4:19 says, *my God will meet all your needs according to his glorious riches in Christ Jesus,* and Ephesians 3:20 says that God *is able to do immeasurably more than all we ask or imagine.* We can't limit God's desires. He is able to do much more than we ask or think He can. We can only limit what He has the power to do through us—what we give Him permission to do. If we don't open ourselves to be His conduits, He will find someone else to work His purposes through—another willing vessel. The "riches in Christ Jesus" are immeasurable. Who are you to try and limit those riches to what you can understand?

Your future is only limited by what you think you can accomplish, within the will of God. If all you can see is being poor, or the current state of your finances, that is how it will remain. If you think you can only be the manager of a fast food restaurant, that is as far as your professional life will go. If you believe God has a higher plan and a larger sphere of influence for you, you will reach it. The key is to dream big, allow God to be the one to open the doors to your future, and above all, do not allow fear to keep you from stepping through those doors!

> **Revival Tip:** *Dream big and allow God to open the doors to your future!*

If you mess up or you cannot grasp the concept of seeing opportunity in the midst of crisis in your heart, it doesn't mean you are not a Christian. You can be a Christian and miss out on your "catch."

In Luke 5:4, Jesus tells Simon, *"Put out into deep water, and let down the nets for a catch."* Simon had a crisis. He had been out with his business partners all day and they had not caught a thing. As a business owner, if I have a totally unproductive day, my business and therefore my livelihood suffers. Jesus was trying to show Simon that all he had to do was obey, even if his request sounded unreasonable. But it was Simon's choice to turn that crisis into an opportunity.

> **Revival Tip:** *What's in your heart determines your future.*

You know the rest of the story. Simon does as Jesus asks, their nets overflow with fish, then he becomes a follower of Jesus. But what was initially in his heart was not a promise of more crisis to come. What was in his heart was obeying Jesus so that he could see how Jesus would turn that crisis into his ultimate opportunity.

What's in your heart determines what's in your future, so it is the wisest idea to carry the promises of God in your heart, where you can "see" them on a regular basis. *For as he thinks in his heart, so is he* (Proverbs 23:7, NKJV).

By What We Say

Numbers 13:26–33 tells the story of Joshua and the other 11 spies who went into the Promised Land. In verse 27, they confirm what God told them about the land, *"We went into the land to which you sent us, and it does flow with milk and honey! Here is its fruit."*

God was right! It was a profitable land. However, then they begin to get scared and speak against their promised future. *[28]But the people who live there are powerful, and the cities are fortified and very large. We even saw descendants of Anak there.* Ten spies all agreed: the land was too dangerous to consider taking.

Nevermind that God was on their side. Nevermind that God was the one who decreed it in the first place. Ten said they would die, and they did die without entering the land. However, two—Caleb and Joshua—said, [30]*"We should go up and take possession of the land, for we can certainly do it."* These two spies were the only ones who entered the Promised Land alive.

> **Revival Tip:** **Whether you say that you can or can't, you will prove yourself right.**

Whether you say you can or can't, ultimately you will prove yourself right. Speak about your future like it's already here today. You may not see the manifestation of it for some time, but by speaking life, you will eventually see life. It took Joshua and Caleb years to see the promise they knew to be true manifest in their lives. Continue saying how things aren't going well for you, how you don't know how to make ends meet, and you will always struggle. Change what you say to be what God wants for you, and you will see increase.

So if you truly want to be successful, if you want to move beyond what your current job allows, you need to first *see* your future as how God says it can be. Then you need to speak it. Open your vision to the endless possibilities He has available to you. Only by taking your limits off of God's ability to work through you will you allow Him to move and change the crises and circumstances of your financial world.

"Who of you by worrying can add a single hour to his life?"

Matthew 6:27

Chapter 4

Poverty

When you hear the word "poverty," what do you think? Do you think of the sponsor-a-child commercials and all the poor tribes in Africa? Do you think of the homeless? Do you think of yourself and your own situation? There is a difference between being impoverished (not having the basic necessities of life: food, shelter, clothing) and living with a spirit of poverty. This chapter may shake your understanding of poverty, but that is a good thing.

Defining Poverty

The spirit of poverty is simply the fear of not having enough, which really is the fear that God will not provide. If you have ever been grocery shopping and worried when you got to the checkout that you wouldn't have enough money to cover your family's grocery needs, that feeling of fear and worry is the spirit of poverty. It is entirely possible to have thousands of dollars in the bank, savings, and investments, and still have a fear that you don't have enough.

> **Revival Tip:** *Poverty is simply the fear of not having enough.*

I have a friend who has a family member that would often help out other family members. She would buy needed things for them like furniture and appliances, and would help with other basic expenses. However, when my friend lost his job, this family member claimed she couldn't help him. My friend knew she had good investments and plenty of money to spend hundreds of dollars on other people, yet she was always complaining and worrying about not being able to pay a bill or her taxes, etc. Even when she would help someone out, she would tell them she was afraid she wouldn't have enough for her needs.

This spirit of fear on my friend's family member is poverty. Despite the actual status of her bank accounts, she still lived in constant fear of not having enough. In this case, the fear of what happened in the past (her family had undergone financial hardship) was contributing greatly to her sense of poverty. In the end, my friend was unable to receive any help from her, which was fine to him, but it tore him up inside when he saw her so worried and fearful when she had plenty to spare. Her fears even rubbed off a little, and my friend began to allow that same spirit of poverty and fear to creep into his life.

What you need to remember when you start worrying about money is, even though it may be true that you don't have much in the bank, God is bigger than you think He is. *Therefore I tell you, do not worry about your life, what you will eat or drink; or about your body, what you will wear. Is not life more important than food, and the body more important than clothes?* ²⁶*Look at the birds of the air; they do not sow or reap or store away in barns, and yet your heavenly Father feeds them. Are you not much more valuable than they?* ²⁷*Who of you by worrying can add a single hour to his life? ...*³³*But seek first his Kingdom and his righteousness, and all these things will be given to you as well* (Matthew 6:25–27, 33).

> **Revival Tip** — **God is bigger than you think He is.**

On top of that, He has already given you everything you need. You may not physically see it yet, but it is there. 2 Peter 1:3 says, *His divine power has given us everything we need for life and godliness through our knowledge of him who called us by his own glory and goodness.*

Stop begging God for things He's already given you, and start being responsible with what you have. If you are unable to pay a bill, yet stopping at Starbucks every day is a necessity of life to you, that is irresponsible. You can cut many practical costs in your daily life and adjust your lifestyle to fit your income. You may not always be able to purchase that hot new cell phone or the latest model car, but not having to worry about if you will have enough to cover your electric bill will be worth it. If you need help creating a lifestyle that fits your income, read my other financial book, *Financial Survival: Practical Ways to Save Money.*

God's Plan

God doesn't want you to beg. He wants you to be the answer to other people's problems. If you can't wrap your head around this concept, you won't allow it to happen. The natural mind is an enemy to your future. You need to stop thinking about your troubles, the money you don't have, and start seeing the possibilities for God to show up in the midst of your circumstances.

> *Revival Tip:* **God wants you to be the answer to other people's problems.**

My husband and I used to beg everyone we knew, and God, for help. At least, to us it felt that way. But when we met a financial counselor who showed us we didn't have to beg God, but simply tap into all He has already promised us, it was a major turning point in our finances.

For the first few months we didn't see any physical change in our bank account. But we did feel a change in our hearts. We began to trust instead of doubt. We had a peace no one could understand. And we still had food on the table, so there was much to be thankful for.

Yes, there were some very tough times as we waited on God's promises, but we held tight to what we knew. We wrote what we knew on the bathroom mirror. We kept a list of His promises that we read every day. By renewing our minds to what He desired for us instead of worrying about *if, when, or how* He was going to provide, it enabled our emotions to calm and we did not have undue stress on our bodies. Romans 12:2 says, *Do not conform any longer to the pattern of this world, but be transformed by the renewing of your mind. Then you will be able to test and approve what God's will is—his good, pleasing and perfect will.*

God's perfect will is not for you to barely survive paycheck to paycheck. He gave humankind the entire earth when it was formed, and an inheritance in Heaven through Jesus' sacrifice. Luke 6:20 says, *Blessed are you who are poor, for yours is the Kingdom of God.* Some Christians take this to mean we are meant to be financially poor and that by somehow always struggling to make ends meet it makes us more holy. However, a few verses later in Luke 6:38 Jesus says, *Give, and it will be given to you. A good measure, pressed down, shaken together and running over, will be poured into your lap.* Why would there be such a contradiction within just a few verses in the same chapter of Luke?

I personally believe the first verse above means that the poor have the opportunity for God to meet their needs above and beyond what they can imagine. And that indeed makes them "blessed." God will get the credit for showing up in the midst of your circumstance. And by forcing the fear back and allowing God to show up, more will be given to you than you could possibly need. This is God's ultimate plan. Not to make us "poor holy Christians," but to take what He blesses us with, which will more than meet our needs, and change the world.

It's a proven fact that it takes finances for a church to function properly. I have been in churches where they weren't sure how they were going to keep the lights on. How can a pastor effectively minister to his congregation, to you, if he is preoccupied with the electric bill? Or the rent? Or the staff's salaries?

> **Revival Tip:** *Money is a tool to reach the world and fulfill the Great Commission.*

If you look at all the ministries that are doing the most to further God's Kingdom here on earth, they all use money to do it. This is a fact of life. We need money to live, but money is not something we should accumulate just to fill our own barns. It is a tool God has given to us to reach the world and fulfill His great commission. See the *Appendix* for a detailed description of what it takes financially for some ministries to fulfill their God-given assignments.

Some people believe that having money is condemned by the Bible. They typically use one verse to prove their point. 1 Timothy 6:10 says, *For the love of money is a root of all kinds of evil. Some people, eager for money, have wandered from the faith and pierced themselves with many griefs.* The key phrase here is, "the love of money." This verse doesn't say money itself is evil, but rather allowing money to take our love and focus away from God is evil.

I ask you this one question. Is it possible to love something to the point it takes you away from a relationship with God, when you are giving that thing away *to* Him and entrusting it to Him on a continual basis?

Jesus came to redeem you from the curse; the curse of poverty being one of many aspects of the larger curse. *For you know the grace of our Lord Jesus Christ, that though he was rich, yet for your sakes he became poor, so that you through his poverty might become rich* (2 Corinthians 8:9). If you insist on believing you're poor, and fearing your financial future, you condemn yourself to a life of poverty no matter what your bank account actually says.

The Curse of Debt

You may have noticed your neighbor's new Jaguar and had a twinge of jealousy. Or maybe one day you drove through an upper-class neighborhood and wished you could live in one of those big, beautiful houses. I used to feel this way myself. In fact, I still struggle with seeing what other people have and wishing I had it.

> **Revival Tip:** *Even Christians have to fight envy.*

Envy is something everyone, even Christians, have to fight on a regular basis. It is forbidden in the 10th commandment (covetousness). When my husband and I met with our first financial counselor at Forward Financial

Group, I brought this up to him. I wanted to know why God blessed others, most noticeably those not respectful to Christ in the world, and not those of us who were serving Him. We were tithing and felt like we were in God's will, yet we were still struggling to make ends meet. At that time, we weren't even buying our own groceries!

Our counselor then told us one of the most profound things I have ever heard. He said not to look at what other people have or didn't have, but *how* they got it. Most of them were probably in debt up to their eyeballs. Some of those big, beautiful houses did not even have furniture in every room, because after paying their massive mortgage payment, the owners couldn't afford any.

> ***Revival* Tip**: **Don't look at what others have, but how they got it.**

When we envy what others have, we get focused on what we don't have rather than what we are blessed with. We become blinded to the gifts God has given us, which have the ability to produce blessing for us and others if we focus on them.

Remember the Parable of the Talents? Matthew Chapter 25 tells the story of how each person was gifted with a different number of talents. One had five, one had two, and the last had one. How they used those talents shows how you can either use what God has given you to increase blessing or keep blessings from coming. For instance, the man with one talent buried it. He did not share his blessing with others, so it did not grow. He was in direct control over how his blessing was used, and he chose to hide it out of fear. The others' talents grew, even doubled, when they invested them. Each person had the same potential to invest their gifts. Each one had the same amount of time to grow their talents.

> **Revival Tip:** *What you do with your gift matters more than just having it.*

Even if you do not have the same gifts as someone else, or the same possessions, what you do with them matters more than having them. Stop looking at what your neighbor has, and begin using what you do have. You may have an incredible talent that can be turned into a business to provide for your family or generate extra income. You may not know much about business, but if you invest your talents into learning what you need to know, your talents will grow.

Recently, I have had the opportunity to visit several multimillion dollar homes. Some of the houses were beautiful, but they all had one thing in common. Instead of their owners using what they already had and growing the talents God had given them, they took matters into their own hands and used massive amounts of debt to get what they wanted. Proverbs 22:7 says, *The borrower is the slave of the lender* (ESV). Think about that. Who do you make your car payment to? What about your mortgage?

What would you be able to do if you didn't have these large payments to lenders?

I know exactly what you're thinking, "But how can I get these things that I need if I don't get a loan? It's too expensive and I don't have the money." I thought the same thing! However, God doesn't want us to pad our lives with beautiful things we don't own. He wants us to learn how to be responsible, have good stewardship with what He has already given us (and be thankful for what we have), and then He will entrust us with more.

> **Revival Tip:** *Whatever you spend money on now, you won't have for something later.*

Think about when you were young and how you handled your allowance (or how your kids handle theirs). Did your parents get upset if you chose to blow your entire allowance on something frivolous? Were they proud if you bought something that was more of an investment? I remember when I was in high school, I wanted to join a music club. It required a monthly payment and I could choose to receive a different music album every month. My parents saw that as responsible. Not only did I have to plan to make sure I had money to cover the next month's issue, but I poured over the contracts of various companies to make sure I got the best deal. A year or so later I ended up canceling that membership, but it taught me something about budgeting and responsibility, which is the lesson God wants each of us to learn so that He can bless us with more.

Now, this doesn't mean you can't ever have that cup of coffee or a pack of gum. Just remember that whatever you spend money on, you will not have that money for something else later. If you have an important purchase to make, you can find a way to get it debt-free.

We recently spent had to spend $2,000 on a new computer for our business. Many people don't have that kind of money sitting around in the bank. In fact, we didn't either. But we had a major need, so I called delinquent accounts to pay up, worked extra hard to get a couple more jobs in, and did what I needed to do to raise the money. It wasn't easy writing out that check, but the benefits of having the new equipment have already paid off. And knowing I didn't have a credit bill looming over my head gave both my husband and me an added peace.

You may not run a business, but maybe you can ask your supervisor for overtime or pick up a second part-time job. Or maybe what you need to do is reevaluate your want and make sure it is something you really need or find something else that will work in its place. Overall, the lesson we learned by overcoming consumer debt and purchasing without loans is that God honors our stewardship. And He has blessed us with more, which we in turn can use to provide for our needs and bless others.

Wouldn't you much rather be servant to a gracious God who does not lend, but gives freely? Or are you content being a slave to the bank and hoping you have that next month's payment when the bill comes?

We have learned that to obey God and do what He says concerning our finances has paid off—literally. Deuteronomy 28:15, 43–44 says, *However, if you do not obey the Lord your God...*[43]*The alien who lives among you will rise above you higher and higher, but you will sink lower and lower.* [44]*He will lend to you, but you will not lend to him. He will be the head, but you will be the tail.* This passage clearly shows that disobeying God's principles concerning your finances will result in poverty. By being "the tail," you will begin to fear not having enough for that next payment. You will always have worry hanging over your head.

> **Revival Tip:** *Debt is a form of modern-day slavery.*

1 Corinthians 7:23 says, *You were bought at a price; do not become slaves of men.* Debt is a form of modern-day slavery. God is calling us to be what Romans 13:8 says—debt-free. *Let no debt remain outstanding, except the continuing debt to love one another, for he who loves his fellowman has fulfilled the law.* As my pastor says, "Jesus paid way too high a price" for you to be a slave to someone else. I know this entire principle goes against everything we are taught, but oftentimes so does God's word. Living within God's established principles has many more benefits than living under the world's financial system.

Even though it may seem that it takes too long for God to answer a prayer when you can get what you want using a credit card, in the long run, waiting is worth it. The reason people use debt is because they don't like waiting. Our culture encourages a "get it now" mentality, when sometimes we are able to obtain bigger blessings if we wait for God's timing. Once you are able to grasp this concept and apply it daily, you will find God actually moves very quickly and all at once.

Let me give you a real-life example of God-timing. It may seem trivial, but a desire of my heart was recently fulfilled. For several years I have wanted a six-speaker stereo system for our TV. I had priced them, but the money would have always been going to something that was more of a necessity. Now, I didn't want this system just for us to use. We enjoy having people over for movies and games, and I love hosting group events. The system would be well used for everyone to enjoy. However, even though I wanted it, I never really told anyone except my husband.

> **Revival Tip**
>
> *When our hearts are right, God can move rather quickly.*

After a while, as we invested more money in the business and I saw the fruits of that, I forgot all about the stereo system. I was too busy working! Once I pretty much gave up on getting anything any time soon and became content with what we already had, a friend asked me if I knew anyone interested in a stereo system. He had one in the trunk of his car and had to get rid of it. He was planning on just giving it away! It turns out this system was almost identical to one of the six-speaker systems I had looked at to purchase. It now resides in our living room. God provided something I wanted, however trivial it may seem, when I became patient with not trying to get it on my own and resorting to debt.

In addition to debt, many people put their hope in government welfare, the chance of winning the lottery, or a game at a casino to prosper them rather than God. The biggest problem with this is, people only have a capacity to handle so much money.

Studies indicate that many lottery winners lose their winnings within five years, file bankruptcy, go deeper into debt, and end up having to live off the same level of income they had before they won. This is because they have not trusted God to increase their capacity for more by being good stewards of what they already have and gaining wealth His way. Poverty has nothing to do with the amount of money one has, but rather one's attitude toward it.

> *Revival Tip*
>
> **Poverty has nothing to do with how much money you have.**

The Battle

You will find that 99.9% of the battle is not going to be with your job or sources of income. It won't be with your creditors or your bills. 99.9% of the battle is in your mind. You must learn to renew your mind, dwell on the promises of God and your right to those promises through what

Jesus did for you on the cross. And continually remind yourself of these facts when the hard financial news hits.

You may have to do some practical things to ease your budget constraints, but until you get your mind working in sync with God's desires for you, those practical things will not allow you to grow beyond merely surviving. It is time to revive your finances through the power of what you think and say, and tap into all that God has for you to accomplish.

"The earth is the Lord's, and everything in it."

Psalm 24:1

Chapter 5

Stewardship

In the last chapter I touched on the concept of stewardship. Now we will delve deeper into what it means in relationship to your finances.

The Cost

Good stewardship isn't being "cheap" or always getting something for nothing. It is about taking care of the vision God's given you, which may be a very big vision. It doesn't always mean you are supposed to get the cheapest "deal." You will have the opportunity to get good deals and you should take advantage of those. But continually being cheap is not good stewardship. Recently I searched the Internet for the phrase, "Christians are cheap." The *second* listing in the search results was a Web site with the heading "You know what's wrong with Christians? They're lousy tippers."

How tragic! This tells you something about how many people view Christianity. They see Christians as cheap, unfair, and unwilling to pay someone what their work is worth.

Unfortunately, this is not a new perception of people who say they follow God. The Pharisees were notorious for being cheap. In Matthew Chapter 23, they claimed they were unable to help provide for their families because they were giving their firstfruits to God. Jesus got very angry and noticed that though they tithed, they were hypocrites because they were ignoring important things like justice, mercy, and faith. Everything they did was for show, and they prided themselves on following the rules to the letter.

> **Revival Tip:** *God expects us to live lives of quality and excellence.*

By not living a life of quality and excellence, it is a reflection on our faith and the God we serve. Do you want to be labeled as someone who doesn't care about others? This is not what Jesus commissioned us to do.

You should not be sacrificing quality in favor of what will cost you the least. After all, lower-cost items often end up costing you much more in the long run. It is often said, "You get what you pay for." A cheap price tag usually translates into items that break down more often or don't deliver what you really need, causing financial, mental, emotional, and even physical strain that you could have avoided by paying for something with lasting value. You can save a lot of money by feeding your family junk food, but is that good for their long-term health?

When my father was young, he drove a Monte Carlo. He saw another car, a Chevette, that looked good on the outside and was cheap, so he traded in his Monte Carlo. My father was told by the salesman that the car had not been in any accidents, but he later discovered it had a bent wheel and axle that was clearly the result of an accident. My father found out that his "cheap deal" was going to cost him a lot more than he planned, and he has not purchased anything based solely on its price since then. This does not mean you can't find bargains. But when bargain hunting, look for quality, not just for the cheapest deal.

God wants you to live a life of excellence. *If anything is excellent or praiseworthy—think about such things* (Philippians 4:8). This doesn't mean that you have to drive a Lexus. What it does mean is that He doesn't want you to purchase something that will not be reliable for your family and will continually break down if you can obtain something better (see 1 Timothy 5:8). This will require you to have a bigger vision for your life and to allow Him, by faith, to open the doors to fulfill that vision.

God wants you to dream so big it will not be possible for your dream to come true without Him. He wants you to rely on Him, not on your own means or creditors. Being faithful to the vision God has given you may cost more than you ever dreamed possible. It most likely will make you rely on His provision to see it through.

The only way you will have the strength to dream as God wants you to dream is to understand and come to the revelation that *you* don't own anything. *The earth is the Lord's, and everything in it, the world, and all who live in it* (Psalm 24:1). God has entrusted the earth to us and everything He gives you is for you to take care of. You need to shift from the mindset of "owner" to "caretaker." And doing that will cost you something. It will cost you a piece of your identity and the ability to take credit when things work out. Yes, you have to give Him the credit. You have to come to the point where you realize He is your source. However, by giving up these desires, you are positioning yourself in a place where God will be able to use you above and beyond what you could do on your own. So the question to ask yourself is, do you value money more than your relationship with God and having His influence on your life?

> **Revival Tip:** *We must shift from the mindset of "owner" to that of "caretaker."*

The Flow

Money will always flow to those who know how to utilize it. This is clear from the Parable of the Talents in Matthew Chapter 25. Use money how God wants you to use it—not just for why you "need" it, but rather why God needs you to have it. Ask yourself this question: "What would I do with $400,000?" If your answer is "buy this for myself" or "I can't fathom that amount of money," then you probably are not ready for God to entrust you with abundant financial provision and blessing. Once you can determine where that flow of money would go and begin to make small commitments to be obedient to what He would have you do with it, God will begin to place you in situations that will enable you to reach more and do more for Him. You must put yourself in a position where God will trust you.

God wants you to have goals. But He wants you to ask Him what His goals are for you, then commit to them, even if they seem beyond reach and especially if they seem beyond your ability. Goals reached are the product of daily commitments. Make those daily commitments—start small—then you will see God begin to trust you with more and more.

When my husband and I moved to start his new job, I started our business again from scratch. I knew this was the call God had placed on my life, and I set small goals to see this vision come to reality. I started with the simple goal of attending one networking event each month to make connections with other businesspeople in the community. Then the goals grew to attending conferences and getting as much training as I could.

> *Revival* Tip — *Each time I work on a God-given goal, things fall into place.*

As I built on what I learned, God began to place people in my path that helped the vision along and gave me new, even bigger goals to accomplish. Each time I work on a God-given goal, things supernaturally fall into place.

Connections I couldn't have dreamed of, provision from people I would never have thought I'd meet, etc. If I try to take matters into my own hands, things quickly fall apart. I know I am working on God-given goals when peace and provision flow through the work of my hands.

The Trap of Debt

Yes, we are going to discuss debt again. Good stewardship does not rely on debt. Trusting in the world's financial system of debt will reap no rewards. Debt only steals from you. I cannot stress this enough. In Judges 6:3–4, the Israelites planted seed, but the harvest was continually stolen. *Whenever the Israelites planted their crops, the Midianites, Amalekites and other eastern peoples invaded the country.* ⁴*They camped on the land and ruined the crops all the way to Gaza and did not spare a living thing for Israel, neither sheep nor cattle nor donkeys.* This is similar to the situation many people find themselves in today. If you are in debt, you are allowing your creditors to steal your harvest.

> *Revival* Tip — **Good stewardship does not rely on debt.**

Do you wonder why God isn't blessing your finances? Do you have a pattern of debt to how you obtain things you want? Do you have credit card balances, car loans, school loans, mortgages? Now, having had student loans myself, and knowing the "good debt" concept behind them, I still am now convinced that any kind of debt steals your harvest. Some people feel you can't get through college without a student loan, or you cannot have a good job without going to college. The fact of the matter is, you can work your way through school, you can make enough money to provide for your children so they do not have to use debt to go to school, and you can get a job, or even start your own business, without a college degree. You can disagree with me if you like, but I believe God's plan is for us to not have to resort to debt for anything.

> **Revival Tip:** *When you're in debt, money is your master.*

You may be tithing and giving offerings, but if you are deep in debt, your lenders are taking your harvest and leaving you little, if anything, to plant again. Matthew 6:24 says, *No one can serve two masters. Either he will hate the one and love the other, or he will be devoted to the one and despise the other. You cannot serve both God and Money.* When you're in debt, money becomes your master. You have payments to make on time and penalties if you don't. Your life begins to revolve around the ability to make your payments. If you did not have these payments, you would be completely free to do what God has called you to do. It is very difficult to be devoted to God and what He is saying concerning your finances and be in debt up to your eyeballs.

Debt is slavery to your lenders, and it makes a way for you to easily get into a position of "biting off more than you can chew." What happens when you take too big of a bite? You choke. It doesn't matter how nutritious that bite is, it can still be fatal. Ephesians 2:1–3 says, *As for you, you were dead in your transgressions and sins, ²in which you used to live when you followed the ways of this world and of the ruler of the kingdom of the air, the spirit who is now at work in those who are disobedient. ³All of us also lived among them at one time, gratifying the cravings of our sinful nature and following its desires and thoughts. Like the rest, we were by nature objects of wrath.*

The way of the world is to gratify the cravings of our sinful nature by using debt as a means to get what we want now, rather than waiting and saving up to purchase what we want debt-free. Unfortunately, too many times when you use debt to get what you want, something better comes along. Suddenly you are swept up into the trap of "keeping up with the Joneses" because it is easy to use debt again after using it the first time.

> **Revival Tip**: *After using debt once, it's even easier to use it again and again.*

Breaking that cycle is extremely difficult, but it is possible. For someone who chokes, there is the Heimlich. For someone deep in debt, there is grace and forgiveness and a chance to pay it off and live debt-free. Even if you are deep in debt as my family was when we first began to learn of God's Kingdom and how it applies to our finances, there is hope! Mark 11:24 has become our family verse:

Therefore I tell you, whatever you ask for in prayer, believe that you have received it, and it will be yours.

That doesn't necessarily mean we are to ask God for that trendy new cell phone, especially if we haven't been responsible to pay our cell phone bills. But it does mean that if you have been a good steward, or in your heart you have made a commitment to God to start living by His ways in your finances, He will provide for your dreams in ways you cannot fathom.

"But seek first his Kingdom and his righteousness, and all these things will be given to you as well."

Matthew 6:33

Chapter 6

Obedience

In the last chapter we discussed good stewardship, which is a form of obedience. God won't tell you what to do next if you haven't done what He's already asked you to do. Clearly He has already asked you to do some things with your finances, like trust Him to provide and be responsible with what He gives you. Trust is not always easy, but it is necessary to walk in all the good promises God has made for your life. If you have accepted Jesus as Savior, you already trust God with your soul—why is it so hard for you to trust Him with your money?

To trust God with your finances, you need to obey His principles regarding tithing (giving 10% of your income to the furthering of God's Kingdom through your church) and giving. We put such a high value on money, so when God's got your wallet, He has *you*. Your obedience opens the door for God's provision to flow unrestrained.

If you find it hard to step out in faith, or you don't possibly see how you can get by on 90% of your paycheck, remember this: God is always discovered in our stepping out on faith. If you do not step out, even if you are uncertain or it hurts, you are not opening a door for God to step through to meet your needs in an amazing and often unpredictable way.

Use What You Have

What you want God to do for you is in your hands already. Exodus 14:14 tells what will happen if you obey with what you already have: *The Lord will fight for you; you need only to be still.* In this passage, Moses and the Israelites have encountered the impossibility of crossing the Red Sea. Many times you encounter impossibilities in the realm of your finances. What did Moses have? What did God ask him to use? All Moses had was his staff, which was nothing except a stick of wood. God had used the staff to work miracles before, and so the people should not have been surprised when God used it again. After all, it was all Moses had on hand—literally.

> *Revival Tip*: **God provides when you reach the realm of impossibility.**

We have to remember that God is the one who told Israel to cross the sea. He led them to the realm of impossibility and turned it into an incredible act of provision. If you will do what God says to do regarding your tithe, you will not only find your immediate impossible needs met (your Red Sea), but you will encounter miracles, perhaps even receiving land you didn't buy, vehicles you didn't purchase, furniture provided where you least expected it, and more. Miracles follow those who dare to trust and use what God has already given them.

> **Revival Tip:** *God will fight for you in your time of need.*

My husband and I have some friends at our church who experienced one of these miracles. They had a death in the family, but the expense to travel to the funeral was too much for them to bear. They prayed over their need, honored God with their tithe, and sowed seed in offerings. Soon their faith and act of obedience was rewarded. Not only were they able to go to the funeral, but everything from the hotel to the rental car, meals, and airfare were 100% covered. They didn't expect to go at all, so every provision that came was miraculous. As they shared this story with me, they also shared how they are still able to tell it as a wonder of living in obedience to God in the realm of their finances and encourage others in the process. They used what they had—their understanding of God's principles, their seed, and their faith—and God honored it. God fought for them in their time of need.

Faith

Sometimes all you have is your faith in God and the knowledge that He has saved you. If that is so, seek Him first and cling to your faith. *For the pagans run after all these things, and your heavenly Father knows that you need them.*

³³But seek first his Kingdom and his righteousness, and all these things will be given to you as well (Matthew 6:32–33). This passage clearly tells us that God is not only aware of your needs and understands them, but He will provide your needs to you. His only condition on this promise is that you seek Him. Trust Him. Have faith in His provision. Give Him the credit when He provides. *Now faith is being sure of what we hope for and certain of what we do not see* (Hebrews 11:1). Faith is all you need.

Faith is like a key to God. If you trust God, you will obey Him regarding your finances. Jesus said it best, *If you love me, you will obey what I command* (John 14:15). Obeying the principles God established of tithing and giving is an act of faith that gives us access to blessings in the Kingdom. This does not mean you tithe or give an offering expecting God to give you something in return. It means that when you tithe, you are releasing control of your finances to God so that He can bless you beyond measure. It means that by tithing you are giving God the credit when miracles happen. It means that if you have a specific desire on your heart, you are allowing Him to fulfill that desire.

Obedience in Tithe

One of the first acts of obedience we take as Christians is to believe in God. But even Satan and demons believe in God. To take it one step further, we need to trust God with everything. If you trust God with your money, you are taking a big step toward trusting Him with everything. Think about it. You go to work. Why? To earn a paycheck—money. You spend money on food, clothing, transportation—the necessities of life. Money is essential.

You probably think about it more than you realize. *For as he thinks in his heart, so is he* (Proverbs 23:7, NKJV). Your thoughts about money position your heart.

God's blessing will flow through you when you obey with tithes and offerings because it is a demonstration of your trust in Him. In Genesis 14:20, the high priest Melchizedek tells Abram, *"And blessed be God Most High, who delivered your enemies into your hand."* Then Abram gave him a tenth of everything. Abram recognized the principle of tithing because he trusted God.

By tithing, or giving 10% of your income to the furthering of God's Kingdom through your church, you are submitting your finances to His authority. Any time you submit to His authority, it brings blessing. When you give, it puts you in a position to let God move in your life, church, and community. I will discuss this more in depth in Chapter 10.

> **Revival Tip:** *If you trust God with your money, you can trust Him with anything.*

You need to know that your tithe is *not* the most important thing. Your obedience is. Tithing has little to do with money, but it has everything to do with the position of your heart—what is important to you. It is also the only area of your Christian life where God has asked you to test Him. Malachi 3:10 says, *"Bring all the tithes into the storehouse, that there may be food in My house, and try Me now in this," says the Lord of hosts, "If I will not open for you the windows of heaven and pour out for you such blessing that there will not be room enough to receive it."* It is clear that God wants us to tithe. It is also obvious that He will provide above and beyond our needs. But obeying in the area of tithing may be difficult at first because it makes you put your money where your mouth is as a Christian. You say you believe, but if you are not tithing, you have not tested the limits of your belief. And if you cannot test the limits of your belief, how do you know what you believe isn't just a "feel-good, get-me-into-Heaven" system rather than God's desire of true belief?

Obedience Yields Results

Deuteronomy 28:2 shows us that God has already promised blessing. *And all these blessings shall come upon you and overtake you, because you obey the voice of the Lord your God.* It is up to us to obey and tap into what He has already set aside. Later in verse 12, we see clearly that we cannot fulfill God's purposes to be the lenders and givers He calls us to be if we are continually borrowing. *The Lord will open to you His good treasure, the heavens, to give the rain to your land in its season, and to bless all the work of your hand. You shall lend to many nations, but you shall not borrow.*

In order to yield good results, you must make sure you're sowing your finances in obedience. Money, just like seed, is useless unless it is sown in fertile soil. There was a time when the Israelites looked after their own needs and desires, didn't tithe, and put off the building of the Lord's house. *This is what the Lord Almighty says: "These people say, 'The time has not yet come for the Lord's house to be built.'"*

³*Then the word of the Lord came through the prophet Haggai:* ⁴*"Is it a time for you yourselves to be living in your paneled houses, while this house remains a ruin?"* (Haggai 1:2–4)

> **Revival Tip:** *Like a seed, money is useless unless it is sown in fertile soil.*

By continually sowing into your own needs and neglecting the tithe, you are hindering God's ability to use the church as He intended. And there is a consequence for disobeying this foundational principle. In verses 6 and 9, *Now this is what the LORD Almighty says: "Give careful thought to your ways. ⁶You have planted much, but have harvested little. You eat, but never have enough. You drink, but never have your fill. You put on clothes, but are not warm. You earn wages, only to put them in a purse with holes in it... ⁹You expected much, but see, it turned out to be little. What you brought home, I blew away. Why?" declares the LORD Almighty. "Because of my house, which remains a ruin, while each of you is busy with his own house."* Here we see that not only will you reap abundant blessings by sowing into the fertile soil of the Lord's house, but you will have His hand of protection on your own house.

You may think you need to look after your own needs first and that the first 10% could be better used for your bills. However, God can do so much more with your 90% than you could alone.

> **Revival Tip:** *God can do so much more with 90% than you can do alone.*

My husband and I were without a steady income for nine months. During that time, we still tithed 10% on every little trickle that came in from odd jobs through our fledgling business. On the bank account statements during that trial, the deductions continually read large amounts: $900 for housing, $300 for the car, $150 for utilities, and so on. The deposits column read: $150 occasionally, $100 here and there, and $50 once in a while. The numbers literally should not have added up!

However, God protected us. Our account didn't go in the negative, and as we learned more about how His economy works (see Chapter 9), we saw real results as those deposit numbers went up. Not only did God protect our bank account, but He protected our health as well. I would get chronic bronchitis, yet I was always able to get the medicine I needed for free. My husband never got sick. Our marriage was not strained to the point of adding stress that we could not handle.

There were many bad days, some moments of hopelessness, but God always provided someone to speak into our lives when we needed it. Looking back, I am very thankful we did not stop tithing. I cannot imagine going through those painful circumstances and trials without God's hand of protection, even if there were moments I didn't "feel" His hand on us in the midst of it all. Obedience is a decision, not a feeling.

Later in Haggai Chapter 1, we see that the people finally chose to obey God's command and began to tithe and build His house. *They came and began to work on the house of the LORD Almighty, their God, [15]on the twenty-fourth day of the sixth month in the second year of King Darius* (Haggai 1:14–15). Then in Haggai 2:18–19, God honors their obedience. *Consider now from this day forward, from the twenty-fourth day of the ninth month, from the day that the foundation of the Lord's temple was laid—consider it: [19]Is the seed still in the barn? As yet the vine, the fig tree, the pomegranate, and the olive tree have not yielded fruit. But from this day I will bless you.*

> **Revival Tip:** Obedience is a decision, not a feeling.

Even though things looked bleak during the time the Israelites tithed, and even shortly after, God promised He would bless them from that day on and He honored that promise. The fruit trees did not have fruit, yet He provided for His people. All because they obeyed. This is the same thing that my family experienced. We tithed, and we thought things still looked bad, but by tithing we were allowing God to bless the other 90% beyond what it was when it was 100%. *If the dough offered as firstfruits is holy, so is the whole lump, and if the root is holy, so are the branches* (Romans 11:16). By tithing that little 10%, that firstfruit, we are declaring that God will make the other 90% that is left holy as well, and therefore it is blessed.

Proverbs 3:9–10 echoes this principle. *Honor the Lord with your possessions, and with the firstfruits of all your increase;* [10]*so your barns will be filled with plenty, and your vats will overflow with new wine.* By honoring God with your firstfruits, your 10%, people will see the results in your life and you will point to God as your provider. Ultimately, He gets all the glory for the provision, as it says in 2 Corinthians 9:13, *As a result of your ministry, they will give glory to God. For your generosity to them and to all believers will prove that you are obedient to the Good News of Christ* (NLT). Your obedience and generosity will lead others to what you know — that God is your source, your provider. The door will open for you to share your heart and passion with them.

> *Revival* Tip — **Your obedience will show others that God is your source and provider.**

Disobedience Yields Results

Obviously if obedience yields the results above, disobedience will yield opposite results. One of the most important results of disobedience you need to be aware of is found in Judges 6:7–10 (NKJV) *And it came to pass, when the children of Israel cried out to the Lord because of the Midianites,* [8]*that the Lord sent a prophet to the children of Israel, who said to them, "Thus says the Lord God of Israel: 'I brought you up from Egypt and brought you out of the house of bondage; ⁹and I delivered you out of the hand of the Egyptians and out of the hand of all who oppressed you, and drove them out before you and gave you their land. ¹⁰Also I said to you, "I am the Lord your God; do not fear the gods of the Amorites, in whose land you dwell." But you have not obeyed My voice."'*

God will not be able to deliver you until you obey His commands. The Israelites had obeyed God's commands in the past, and they should have remembered all God had already done for them. But just as they forgot, we tend to forget.

> *Revival Tip*: **Keep track of the times when God steps in when you obey Him.**

It is very important for you to keep a record of times when God stepped in, when you obeyed, or when you stepped out in faith and He came through with a miracle—however small that miracle was. By keeping a record of this, you can look back at the benefits of obedience and make a clearer decision when you feel like disobeying and not giving the tithe.

Sometimes that 10% will hurt. Many times it will feel like a choice between obedience and food for your family. But whenever you obey, the food will supernaturally be provided. God always takes care of those who honor Him!

Authority

In order to understand why we must be obedient to God's commands, we need to understand how God set up authority on the earth. There were many times when my family couldn't understand why God didn't just intervene in our situation. Couldn't He see we were hurting? Didn't He understand we had no food to eat? Why, if He sees the need, won't He just step in and fix it?

Much of the reason why He couldn't just step in and fix our needs had to do with authority. In the beginning, God gave man all authority on the earth. This meant we had the power to control it. However, when man fell into sin by disobeying God, that authority transitioned from Adam and the human race to Satan.

> **Revival Tip** — *God had another plan for returning authority to humanity.*

Luke 4:5–6 says, *The devil led [Jesus] up to a high place and showed him in an instant all the kingdoms of the world. ⁶And the devil said to him, "All this authority I will give You, and their glory; for this has been delivered to me, and I give it to whomever I wish."* Here, Satan is gloating that he has been given authority and splendor over the earth. This happened during Adam's sin, when he and Eve gave in to Satan's temptation. In turn, Satan here was now tempting Jesus with that authority. After all, Jesus was wholly man,

Chapter 6: Obedience

and the authority was rightfully Satan's to return to man or give to whomever he chose.

However, we know what Jesus knew. God had another plan for returning authority to humanity. It meant a great deal of pain, physical and spiritual, but it was the right way and Jesus knew it. So He suffered, died, rose again, and as a result all authority on earth was given to Him.

Then Jesus came to them and said, "All authority in heaven and on earth has been given to me. [19]Therefore go and make disciples of all nations, baptizing them in the name of the Father and of the Son and of the Holy Spirit, [20]and teaching them to obey everything I have commanded you. And surely I am with you always, to the very end of the age." (Matthew 28:18–20). By Jesus giving the Great Commission to His disciples before physically leaving the earth in verse 19, He has transferred that authority back to humanity.

By tithing, we voluntarily use our authority to allow God to move circumstances on our behalf and place us under His divine protection. *"I will prevent pests from devouring your crops, and the vines in your fields will not cast their fruit," says the Lord Almighty* (Malachi 3:11). Through Jesus' sacrifice, we have legal dominion on the earth and over Satan. We just need to take hold of it. *Submit yourselves, then, to God. Resist the devil, and he will flee from you* (James 4:7).

We have authority on the earth. Until we use it, heaven's power will not be released in our world. We have the keys to bind and loose. *I will give you the keys of the Kingdom of heaven; whatever you bind on earth will be bound in heaven, and whatever you loose on earth will be loosed in heaven* (Matthew 16:19).

Bind the enemy instead of putting up with circumstances the way they are now. Then loose the provision of Heaven into your world. Through grace, God has blessed you, and by your obedience you allow that blessing to flow into your life. You have the authority to do that, and the means to do it are through trusting God with your finances—especially when it hurts. Try it and watch God show up!

"A good man leaves an inheritance for his children's children."

Proverbs 13:22

Chapter 7

Prosperity

Let me assure you right off the bat, this chapter is not about the so-called "prosperity doctrine." I am not of the belief that people are meant to hoard treasures for themselves on earth. However, you need to know the definition of true prosperity, as God sees it, and its purpose in your life before you can really grasp what He wants for your finances.

Prosperity Is God's Idea

Prosperity as God sees it is like a water main supplying water to a city. Without an adequate supply, the city will dry up. Have you ever experienced a drought? Usually water is rationed in a drought until rain fills the reservoirs again. Who provides the rain? Who created it? God!

If you wish to understand prosperity as God defines it, you need to understand the power of being a "water main," or conduit. Just as with no rainwater a city will thirst, without the conduit it will have no way of reaching that water supply it so desperately needs. God's power and provision is the supply. You are the conduit. Without you, God's supply will not reach your city. Without God prospering you—moving His provision through you—your position as a conduit will dry up and be useless.

> **Revival Tip:** *Prosperity was originally God's idea.*

Prosperity was originally God's idea! Even in the Garden of Eden, God provided everything humankind would need to not only live, but thrive and prosper. Everything we could have ever needed was given to us at the beginning. A very popular verse, Jeremiah 29:11 says, *"For I know the plans I have for you,"* declares the Lord, *"plans to **prosper** you and not to harm you, plans to give you hope and a future."* Luke 12:32 also says, *For your Father has been pleased to give you the Kingdom.* As God sees it, He is pleased to prosper you, to give you everything in His Kingdom, which includes earthly possessions so that you can accomplish His purposes here on earth. *Let the Lord be magnified, Who has pleasure in the prosperity of His servant* (Psalm 35:27).

Prosperity Leads to Influence

In order to have influence, you must have prosperity. By God prospering us, we are enabled to influence others. If you have a spiritual influence (God working through you), it will always result in a natural influence. For instance, I have personally prayed for the healing of people with allergies. Having experienced healing myself, I asked God to prosper my healing to the point I could be a conduit of healing for others. When I prayed for them, I could literally feel the power of God flow through my arms to the people, even if I didn't touch them. Some of them had a noticeable improvement in their health after I prayed for them. This is a practical example of how God's touch prospered my health and led to my ability to influence the health of others. If He had not prospered my health first, I would not have anything to give the ones I prayed for. And if He had the desire to heal me, surely He wanted others to experience healing as well.

Just as I believe God desires everyone to live in full health, He also wants to prosper our finances. Proverbs 13:22 says, *A good man leaves an inheritance for his children's children.* This is God's plan for your prosperity. He wants you to prosper so much, your grandchildren benefit from it. His plan is not for everyone to grow up, go to college, go into massive amounts of debt, then spend the bulk of their adult lives paying back that debt, barely being able to put their own kids through school. He would rather see you prosper to the point your children and their children are provided for.

> *Revival Tip* — ***In order to have influence, you must have prosperity.***

Think of this: if you were provided for by your parents, how much more of a difference could you make in the lives of others? If you had no debt payments, how could you use your money to help those in need? It is not about spoiling your children or grandchildren. It is about making sure their needs are met as well as teaching them to be responsible with what they are given so that they can freely act on the dreams and visions God has entrusted to them.

As God sees it, He has to prosper you in order for you to fulfill His purpose for your life of being a provision for others. In Genesis 12:2, He makes a promise to Abram: *I will make you into a great nation and I will bless you; I will make your name great, and you will be a blessing.* The key phrase here is "and you will be a blessing." God is not prospering your finances just so you can be comfortable, live in a large house, have expensive cars, and eat at the finest restaurants. Some of that may happen, but His number one goal is to make you an influencer.

> **Revival Tip:** *God's goal is to make you an influencer.*

The amount of influence you have to carry out God's purposes is directly related to your relationship with Him. Your proximity in relationship to God and openness of heart to what He has for you will determine the amount of influence you carry. The closer you become to God and the more you seek His purpose for your life, the more your trust in Him will grow and the more He will be able to place people and opportunities in your path to create influence.

You must also be close in proximity to the people you're influencing to effectively reach them. Yes, you can influence strangers. But how much greater is the influence if you have a relationship with the person you are helping? My husband and I have had the opportunity to help someone buy groceries, fill a friend's gas tank, and more. But it meant more to them because we already had a relationship with them. They knew we did not expect anything in return. We simply paid attention to the nudge God put in our hearts to influence them and chose to act on it. Because God had blessed and prospered us, and since we had been in their shoes before and understood what they needed, we had the ability to influence them in a practical way. By being that conduit to fill their need, we have enabled them to have a testimony of God's provision in the midst of their circumstances.

When my family was on the brink of losing everything and we had sold as much as we could just to get by, we had trouble taking what we saw as "charity" from those of influence. However, now I see that God has another plan. By allowing someone to influence us, we not only had a testimony of how God provided in the midst of our circumstances, but the person who helped us was blessed in return. *And remember the words of the Lord Jesus, that He said, "It is more blessed to give than to receive"* (Acts 20:35).

By being a good steward of what God had blessed them with, He entrusted them with more. If you have trouble accepting "charity" from others, ask yourself this question: who are you to deny God's blessing on their lives? By not accepting their gifts, you are keeping them from the blessing God has for them. On the other hand, by not listening to those "God-nudges" and therefore not influencing others with the blessings He has given you, you are not allowing them to carry a testimony of His supernatural provision. You carry a supply that is meant for someone else.

> **Revival Tip:** *You carry a supply that is meant for someone else.*

Don't shrink back from God elevating you to a place of influence! He wants to elevate us to the place of influence where we can see and hear clearly. Have you ever climbed a mountain? The view at the top is so much different than below. While at the bottom you can see the vegetation, the wildlife, and the trail. At the top, you get a view of the entire lay of the land.

It is the same way with influence. The greater the influence God gives you, the more of His plan you will be able to see—in your life and others' lives. As you allow God to work in your life, He will change you so that He can change your city and the people around you. If you allow yourself to be open to the possibility, God will move you into a lifestyle of blessing and generosity.

God wants us to be water mains, not little buckets. You may be happy with your small bucket of provision, but it will take a water main of supply to reach the lost and hurting with the love of God. The lost don't always come to church—many times we have to go to them. And that usually takes finances (see *Appendix*). God wants to use your financial situation to be a light in the darkness for others to see.

Light displaces darkness; darkness doesn't displace light. You cannot displace much darkness with a candle. It is better to use a high-powered flashlight. Essentially, to be an effective influencer, you need more power. If you are ready to dive into this new world of influence, you need to keep God as the focus and attribute Him as your source. Then your sphere of influence will only grow. *But remember the Lord your God, for it is he who gives you the ability to produce wealth* (Deuteronomy 8:18).

Prosperity God's Way

Prosperity God's way means He will give you the ability to acquire the things you need, not necessarily the means to purchase them. This has happened to my husband and me many times, most recently with something as simple as bedroom furniture. At the time I wrote this book, my husband and I had been married for eight years. In all those years we only had functioning bedroom furniture for a few months. We have mostly used boxes, under-bed storage units, and a wire rack of drawers a friend found off someone's trash pile to store our clothes.

We began asking God for provision in the way of furniture. It sounds simple, but we were not willing to go into debt to get it, and a nice, quality set of bedroom furniture is not cheap. We tried saving up for the furniture, but more important things would come up and we would have to use the money for something else. We were also giving into God's Kingdom as we saw that as a more important use of our finances than fulfilling our own desires. So we continued to sow into God's Kingdom, believing that His hand would prosper us and bring supernatural provision in the specific area of a simple need—bedroom furniture.

> **Revival Tip:** *God will supply the desires of your heart.*

Then we were given the opportunity to move into a fully furnished home. The furniture is similar to the style I had wanted, but it is a higher quality than we could have afforded to purchase. Not only was bedroom furniture provided, but some much-needed office furniture as well. By sowing into God's Kingdom, He provided in a way we did not see coming. And since the furniture came with the house, we did not have to pay extra for it. Now every time someone visits and comments about the nice furniture, we can tell the story of God's supernatural provision.

We also have the opportunity to share other ways He is prospering us, which has grown our faith through the telling, and theirs through the listening. If you give your heart to sowing into God's Kingdom, you'll naturally reap God's provision and receive things you never thought you would be able to have or afford.

As God supplies the desires of your heart, you need to be willing to live with the things you didn't work for. For example, God told the Israelites, *So I gave you a land on which you did not toil and cities you did not build; and you live in them and eat from vineyards and olive groves that you did not plant* (Joshua 24:13).

Your blessing will be so big you won't be able to handle it and you will have to share it with others. But as a natural result, there will always be plenty for you. This is evident in Luke 6:38, *Give and it will be given to you. A good measure, pressed down, shaken together and running over, will be poured into your lap. For with the measure you use, it will be measured to you.* In the same way you give, you will receive. When rainwater flows down a hill to fill a reservoir, the grass and trees on that hill naturally benefit from the supply of water as it flows to the reservoir. They drink their fill, and the flow continues on to benefit the community.

> **Revival Tip:** *Your blessing will be so big, you won't be able to contain it.*

If others see what God has provided for you and start condemning you for it, remember, you are not the one who worked for those things. In my personal situation, God has provided some things that my husband and I have desired in ways we never planned. His blessing has made us "rich," and I am grateful for having the things He has provided.

I know that at any moment we may be asked to give what He has given us to someone else. And it will be that much easier to pass it on knowing it did not come from our own hands, our hard work, or our sweat to begin with, but from God's desire to bless and prosper us.

Prosperity Gives God Glory

God's blessing, His favor, is on you. In 2 Corinthians 6:2, Paul says, *For [the Lord] says, "In the time of my favor I heard you, and in the day of salvation I helped you." I tell you, now is the time of God's favor, now is the day of salvation.* As Jesus said about Himself in Luke 4:18–19, *The Spirit of the Lord is on me, because he has anointed me...*[19]*to proclaim the year of the Lord's favor.* God's favor includes provision in the midst of difficult circumstances and material blessing. Proverbs 10:22 says, *The blessing of the Lord brings wealth, and he adds no trouble to it.* God does not desire to give you trouble or difficult circumstances, but there will be opposition from the enemy that does not want to see you walking in all God has for you. In addition to being open to what God has for your life, you need to be aware of the opposition to His will coming to pass.

> *Revival Tip:* **When you walk in favor, you will be attacked. So stand firm!**

Any time there's favor on your life, someone will try to attack you and destroy your faith. In the biblical story of Shadrach, Meshach, and Abednego, we see that although they were appointed to a high position of authority by Daniel, who was favored by the king, and were honoring and obeying God's commands, they faced considerable opposition. They were told, *...you must fall down and worship the image of gold that King Nebuchadnezzar has set up. ⁶Whoever does not fall down and worship [the image of gold] will immediately be thrown into a blazing furnace* (Daniel 3:5–6). I would say being burned up in a furnace is some serious opposition! They chose to worship and obey God rather than the king, so they were thrown into a furnace. However, God met them in the midst of their circumstance and provided a way out.

> **Revival Tip:** *It starts with God, not with you.*

Later Daniel himself (Daniel Chapter 6), though in a favored position, was cast into the lion's den for obeying God. God provided for him as well, and as a result, He was elevated to an even higher position in the kingdom. Even though he faced terrible circumstances, he walked in God's favor and prospered.

Deuteronomy 8:18 says, *But remember the Lord your God, for it is he who gives you the ability to produce wealth, and so confirms his covenant, which he swore to your forefathers, as it is today.* We have the ability to be successful, but we need to remember that God is the one who is our source of blessing. *The Lord will send a blessing on your barns and on everything you put your hand to* (Deuteronomy 28:8). By God blessing everything and being your source, giving you His favor and prospering you, He gets the credit for your success.

It starts with God, not with you. Making you great makes God look great. God gets His will done through *you*. Your purpose belongs to Him, and only through Him will you be able to accomplish the amazing things He has planned. It is an adventure. Are you ready to prosper?

"Whoever sows sparingly will also reap sparingly, and whoever sows generously will also reap generously."

2 Corinthians 9:6

Chapter 8

Generosity

Throughout the Bible, we find many references to generosity. What is generosity? Why do some people hang on to what they have, while others give freely, even if sometimes they don't seem to have enough to meet their own needs? Why is the spirit of generosity so important to God?

You Reap What You Sow

In 2 Corinthians Chapter 9, we hear Paul speak about what God asks of us in our finances. 2 Corinthians 9:6–8 says, *Whoever sows sparingly will also reap sparingly, and whoever sows generously will also reap generously. ⁷Each man should give what he has decided in his heart to give, not reluctantly or under compulsion, for God loves a cheerful giver. ⁸And God is able to make all grace abound to you, so that in all things at all times, having all that you need, you will abound in every good work.*

In verse 6, we see that what we reap is directly tied to what we sow. In verse 7, it is clear that the amount we choose to give is up to us. God has set a principle in motion of 10% (see Chapter 10), but I believe this verse is talking about above and beyond the tithe.

We are called to be generous in all things: our time, our resources, and our money. Your generosity is what ultimately will change people's hearts. It will show others that you genuinely care about them. You have probably heard the phrase "actions speak louder than words." Your actions of generosity will cause people to ask you about your faith more than you just telling them about it. Verse 8 makes it clear that God has the power to reward you for your generosity. Not for your own gain, but so your works will reap fruit for His Kingdom.

> **Revival Tip:** *We are called to be generous—in all things.*

Sowing Makes You Rich

Later in 2 Corinthians 9:10–12, as the Apostle Paul states, we see that we are made rich when we are generous. *He who supplies seed to the sower and bread for food will also supply and increase your store of seed and will enlarge the harvest of your righteousness.* [11]*You will be made rich in every way so that you can be generous on every occasion, and through us your generosity will result in thanksgiving to God.* [12]*This service that you perform is not only supplying the needs of God's people but is also overflowing in many expressions of thanks to God.*

I don't know how Paul could have made this any clearer or more obvious. By what's written in verse 10, we see that everything comes from God. He is our source, our supply. It is He who multiplies our seed when we sow, and He who brings the harvest into our lives. Verse 11 shows our reward. We will be enriched for our generosity. The second half of that verse also makes it clear that we are not made rich simply for our benefit, but so that through our reward people will thank God. That is further clarified in verse 12.

The purpose of our tithe and offerings (offerings are covered more in-depth in Chapter 11) is not only so that a ministry's needs can be met. This is not about keeping the air conditioning on and a comfortable environment for churchgoers. The purpose is clearly defined to be so others may see the overflow of financial provision so that the body of Christ can reach even more people who will ultimately give thanks to God and recognize Him as their supply.

> **Revival Tip:** *We will be enriched for our generosity.*

Generosity Is a Principle

Even people who do not have a relationship with God understand the principle of generosity. Many millionaires began making their money when they were giving much of it away. In his book *The Top 10 Distinctions Between Millionaires and the Middle Class,* Keith Cameron notes that one of the distinctions is that millionaires are generous givers. It sounds completely backward from what we are taught. The media teaches us to spend. Investors and financial planners teach us to save. But many people have lost thousands of dollars by either spending what they didn't have or putting their money in risky investments. Though it is important to save, and especially to have an emergency fund, that does not give us the right to neglect what God asks us to give when He asks us to give it.

I have a friend who was led to take money out of her retirement account and invest in something directly related to God's call on her life and purpose. At first, she was ridiculed by her peers for doing "the unthinkable." But after the markets crashed in 2008 and 2009 and many people lost their investments, she kept hers because she followed the direction God laid on her heart.

> **Revival Tip:** *The best investments are made in God's Kingdom.*

Ultimately, the best place to invest is in God's Kingdom. *Do not store up for yourselves treasures on earth, where moth and rust destroy, and where thieves break in and steal.* [20]*But store up for yourselves treasures in heaven, where moth and rust do not destroy, and where thieves do not break in and steal.* [21]*For where your treasure is, there your heart will be also* (Matthew 6:19–21). Giving away your increase doesn't sound smart, by the world's standards. But in my own experience, every time my husband and I gave when we felt led by God, we never once regretted it.

> **Revival Tip:** *When sowing, we have to learn how to trust and be patient.*

This doesn't mean you abandon an emergency fund, savings, or all of your retirement accounts. What it does mean is that when you invest in God's Kingdom, He can send a harvest above and beyond what you would get from worldly investments.

Here is a practical example. I had the opportunity to sow into a guest speaker's ministry at my church. I struggled with doing it, and the amount I felt I could afford was drastically different from what I felt God was telling me to give. However, I had yet to regret sowing into another person's ministry, so I gave the amount God laid on my heart out of our business account. I had large bills coming that next week and no new prospective clients on the horizon. I did not know how I would pay these bills, especially if I gave some of the money set aside to pay them away. But I gave anyway.

The next day, I received three calls for meetings with new clients, and two more existing clients sent me a list of projects they wanted done. God took my meager seed and almost immediately I saw a harvest! What started out as a $150 seed and a prayer turned into $4,000 worth of business within the next week.

Now this doesn't mean that when you sow God will immediately send your harvest. My husband and I have had to learn to trust and be patient, as in the past we didn't see it right away. And sometimes your harvest may not be in the form you expect, but it will always be what you need to fulfill God's purpose. We have learned to give generously, with a grateful and cheerful heart, and to be patient for God to fulfill our harvest. He always will.

"And call upon me in the day of trouble; I will deliver you, and you will honor me."

Psalm 50:15

Chapter 9

God's Economy

Let's get something straight right away. We live in the world. The world's economy does affect us. We need to be aware of what is going on, but we also need to understand that as children of God we have the ability to live in God's economy, which supersedes the world's economy, through our faith.

God's economy operates differently than the world's. For one thing, God works on a totally different time schedule than the world. He also asks some things of us that might not make sense to the world. When you hear all the doom and gloom of the economy on the news and find yourself focusing on the negative and getting depressed, it is time to turn off the TV. Start filling yourself with what God says about your situation and find out what He wants of you.

God doesn't have a problem with you having money. He just wants to know how you will use it. How are you participating in God's business? Will you question Him when He asks something of you? In Isaiah 45:11 (ESV) the Lord says, *Ask me of things to come; will you command me concerning my children and the work of my hands?* When He is working on a level we cannot see, will you question

His motives? God needs you to have money. If you can't see His need for your money, you won't understand how some Christians have the wealth they have. But beyond God needing you to have money, He needs you to be responsible. If you don't completely understand this concept, go back and reread Chapter 5.

> **Revival Tip:** *Do you question God's motives when He asks something of you?*

In the Midst

Probably the biggest hindrances we face in life will be our circumstances. Many of the difficult circumstances you face will probably have something to do with money. Some teachings have said that once you become a Christian, your painful circumstances will immediately disappear. Though this may happen, it is not common. Jesus said, *In this world you will have trouble. But take heart! I have overcome the world* (John 16:33).

God wants to meet you in the middle of your tough circumstances, *not* necessarily get you out of them right away. *You prepare a table before me in the presence of my enemies* (Psalm 23:5). In this passage, David is declaring that although he is surrounded by his enemies, he can sit down to a feast right in front of them. Shouldn't he be hunkered down, hanging on to his weapons, anxiously trying to figure out how he's going to get out of this mess?

Chapter 9: God's Economy

When you have encountered a job loss, a loss of investments, or some other financial hardship, have you tended to grab a hold of everything and hang on tight? Were you anxious about the future? Did you cry out to God to deliver you, to provide the solution for you? Did you get mad if you didn't see the solution right away? When things don't seem to work out, what are you giving your attention to? In our humanity, we tend to react rather than patiently see what God has in store. We want resolution; it's built into us. But God wants to stand with you in the midst of the storm. God wants you to *be still and know that [He] is God* (Psalm 46:10). He wants you to declare Him as your source.

> **Revival Tip** — **God wants to meet you in the middle of your circumstances.**

Another reason God wants to visit you in the *midst* of a problem is because others will take notice. In Daniel 3:28, when God met Shadrach, Meshach and Abednego inside the fiery furnace, *Nebuchadnezzar said, "Praise be to the God of Shadrach, Meshach and Abednego, who has sent his angel and rescued his servants! They trusted in him and defied the king's command and were willing to give up their lives rather than serve or worship any god except their own God."* God did not rescue them from going into the fire, but He showed up in the fire and the king and all those witnessing noticed.

Does it strike you as odd that the king of Babylon would humble himself to the point of admitting he was wrong—in public? It took a drastic approach—God meeting believers in the midst of their storm—to get his attention. Sometimes when you are encountering a storm, God's plan is to use your circumstance to reach someone else who will not listen any other way.

Many times we allow doubt to affect the way we react to a situation. Often it appears in what may seem like the innocent voice of "wonder"—"I wonder if..." Sometimes I have said things like, "I wonder if God really wants me to be successful" or "I wonder if God is going to meet me in this situation." There should be no *ifs* with believers. We need to learn how to see with our hearts—to tap into what God sees. That is faith. The enemy will do everything in his power to distract you or get you to blame God for your crisis. When the storm hits, as it surely will, remember that if the enemy can rob you from hearing and seeing what God has to say, he wins. Hang on to what you know—that God is your supply and He will meet you in the midst—even when you can't see it with your natural eyes. *God is our refuge and strength, an ever-present help in trouble* (Psalm 46:1).

> **Revival Tip:** **Don't allow doubt to affect the way you react.**

The voice of "wonder" also tends to appear when we think we deserve punishment for something. "I wonder if this is happening because I did ____ yesterday." Know that bad circumstances do not occur to teach you a lesson.

They just happen as a result of the fallen world we live in. (See *Authority* in Chapter 6, or for a great article explaining this concept in depth, see Andrew Womack's teaching on *The Sovereignty of God* at his Web site: www.awmi.net). Bad circumstances are an opportunity for God's power to be revealed, either by delivering us out of the trials or supporting us through them. God's words—His promise, what you *know*—will be more sustaining than the circumstance you are in.

> **Revival Tip** — *Settle the issue of trust.*

If you find yourself in bad financial circumstances and do not have enough money to live off of, but you do have enough for a seed (see Chapter 8, *Generosity*), I dare you to defy everything the world's economists are telling you, believe God, and plant it into His Kingdom. *Restore our fortunes, O Lord, like streams in the Negev. ⁵Those who sow in tears will reap with songs of joy. ⁶He who goes out weeping, carrying seed to sow, will return with songs of joy, carrying sheaves with him* (Psalm 126:4–6). In this passage, the people had a circumstance. They lost their fortunes, including their harvests. All they had left was a little seed. They were literally weeping as they sowed what little they had. If you have enough for a seed, but not enough to live off of, plant that seed. It will grow and you will not only have enough of a harvest for your family, but enough to plant again.

It is time to settle an issue. The issue is *trust*. Once you settle that in your spirit, you will be better equipped to weather the next storm. You will know that He is your provider, and that He is with you in the midst of what you are going through.

God Provides What You Need

We all have financial needs. God knows this and has promised to supply not *some*, but *all* of them, if we seek Him first (Matthew 6:33). Every time we honor God with good stewardship and allow Him to meet us in the midst of our circumstances, He will provide for our needs, and many times His provision will be above and beyond what we actually need.

> *Revival* Tip — *God did not promise to supply **some** of your needs, but **all**.*

Honor God, as He is the one who fills your barns to overflowing (Proverbs 3:10). Honor Him by using what He provides to you as a blessing for others. By doing so, by seeking Him first, you will have provision for your needs as well. If everyone in the church does what they are supposed to do, the government won't have to step in to take care of people.

Jesus commissioned His followers to be the ones to bless and help others, not the world's governments. So the next time you have a chance to be a blessing, even if it is simply to lend a listening ear or be a support, don't neglect the opportunity. Taking action on your God-given opportunity will bring provision to you as well. Keep in mind that God does not "need" our money. We should give it willingly to release our finances into His hands. Only by doing this will we tap into God's Kingdom principles and have access to His economy.

> **Revival Tip:** *God does not need our money.*

Types of Provision

There are several ways God uses to provide. He may work a miracle. This has happened in my life when I have been instantly healed, and no longer had to spend money on medications. It has also happened when my husband and I received a check from someone anonymously through our church. Miracles can also happen when God gives us just enough to get through the next day. *And when they measured it by the omer, he who gathered much did not have too much, and he who gathered little did not have too little. Each one gathered as much as he needed* (Exodus 16:18). In the instance of manna, if the people gathered more to hoard, it would turn into worms by morning and be useless. God was testing them to see if they would follow His commands and only gave them what they needed to sustain themselves each day.

Some needs we must take responsibility to step out and get. Think about this: God put all the worms and bugs on the earth that birds will eat. But He does not drop the food directly into their nests. It is up to them to hunt it, find it, and bring it back for their families. When God supplied manna for the Israelites, they were the ones who had to go outside and gather it. It did not supernaturally appear in their bowls every morning. They had to do something to get it (Exodus 16:4).

> **Revival Tip:** *It is up to you to harvest what God has given you.*

It is up to you to harvest what God has given you. If I had not returned the phone calls and emails of those new clients from the story in the previous chapter, or set appointments with them, I would not have secured the harvest that God had so obviously provided. You cannot be wallowing in self-pity so much that you fail to see what God has laid before you.

Another way God provides is extravagantly—with more than enough. Joshua 5:11–12 gives us an example of this: *The day after the Passover, that very day, they ate some of the produce of the land: unleavened bread and roasted grain.* [12]*The manna stopped the day after they ate this food from the land; there was no longer any manna for the Israelites, but that year they ate of the produce of Canaan.* One day the Israelites were still being sustained daily with manna, but the next they finally ate the produce of the Promised Land, which was abundantly overflowing (Numbers 13).

"More than enough" is what we are called to live under. *"Bring the whole tithe into the storehouse, that there may be food in my house. Test me in this," says the Lord Almighty, "and see if I will not throw open the floodgates of heaven and pour out so much blessing that you will not have room enough for it. ¹¹I will prevent pests from devouring your crops, and the vines in your fields will not cast their fruit," says the Lord Almighty. ¹²"Then all the nations will call you blessed, for yours will be a delightful land," says the Lord Almighty* (Malachi 3:10–12).

Provision is waiting for us. All we have to do is participate in the principles of God's economy. When we give God permission to touch our finances, His touch delivers and increases us. *And call upon me in the day of trouble; I will deliver you, and you will honor me* (Psalm 50:15).

> **Revival Tip** — **We are called to live under more than enough.**

Faith

The world's economy demands your money. Think about it. There are advertisements everywhere. You cannot even go to the grocery store without being bombarded by ads on TVs hanging from the ceiling, on the walls and end caps, even on the floors themselves! It is true that we need things like housing, gas, food, and clothing. But God will take care of all these things when we honor Him first.

Probably the largest factor that determines our ability to tap into God's economy is faith. It is a constant fight to stay in faith. Hebrews 11:1 says, *Now faith is being sure of what we hope for and certain of what we do not see.* Even if you can't feel it, you know God has provided it for you. You may not see it, but you are sure it is there. That is faith.

> **Revival Tip** — *Staying in faith requires a constant fight.*

In 2006, my family's faith was tested in a major way. After years of struggling to make ends meet and searching for a steady job, my husband made a list of what he needed in a new job and began praying over it every day. Shortly after, he landed an interview at a publishing company. The job description matched what we were praying for, and we knew in our hearts that this was his job. However, after the interview, an entire month passed without us hearing anything. If you have ever been job hunting, you know that typically when that much time goes by the job has probably gone to someone else. Especially in the case of his competitive field, we felt like the job's manifestation was not going to happen.

We asked the financial counselor who had introduced us to the principles of God's economy for his advice. He told us something that has stuck with us ever since. He reminded us that this job was God's provision for us. We had faith that it met every need we had written down and was going to be his. It just hadn't manifested yet. Our counselor said that even if the job went to someone else, it would not work out for them because this job was designated for my husband.

What he told us may sound odd to you, but looking back it makes perfect sense. We pressed through and kept believing God's promise even though we didn't see it. Three months after his initial interview, we moved to North Carolina and my husband began his new job.

There was a point during that three-month period when we struggled with despair. We were completely uncertain why God was taking so long to fulfill His promise to us. I believe that if we had succumbed to the despair and hopelessness we felt, even though the feelings were real, what needed to be moved in the spiritual realm for the job to manifest in our natural world would not have happened.

> *Revival Tip* — **Faith moves things from spiritual to natural.**

Faith moves things from spiritual to natural and doubt and despair are the opposite of faith. *"Have faith in God," Jesus answered. "I tell you the truth, if anyone says to this mountain, 'Go, throw yourself into the sea,' and does not doubt in his heart but believes that what he says will happen, it will be done for him"* (Mark 11:23). With the support of each other and others, we kept believing and declared God's promise several times each day. After making it through this challenging time, things happened very quickly. Two weeks later my husband had an in-person interview, was offered the job, and we were packed and moving.

> **Revival Tip:** *Keep hanging on to the promise you were given.*

When you press through, you must keep hanging on to the promise you are given—what you know God is saying and what you are believing for. Your faith must persevere until you see it begin to happen, no matter how long it takes. Don't give up! Giving up means using the credit cards to get something you are believing God for, taking matters into your own hands, or surrendering yourself to doubt and depression.

Sometimes when you are at your lowest point, as we were, you must go back to the beginning of what you know God said and promised to you. If all you know for sure is that Jesus has saved you, then start there. You will be reminded of His other promises, right up to the one you are currently believing for. And when you are reminded of all the promises He has already fulfilled, your faith will increase so that you can persevere until this next promise is manifest in your life.

Chapter 9: God's Economy

An example of this act of perseverance can be found in the book of Daniel. The moment Daniel prayed, an angel was dispatched with an answer to his prayer. But the angel wrestled with the enemy for 21 days before he arrived. The angel told him, *"Do not be afraid, Daniel. Since the first day that you set your mind to gain understanding and to humble yourself before your God, your words were heard, and I have come in response to them.* ¹³*But the prince of the Persian kingdom resisted me twenty-one days. Then Michael, one of the chief princes, came to help me, because I was detained there with the king of Persia"* (Daniel 10:12–13).

Daniel persevered during that 21 days until his answer came. Faith, added to perseverance, equals us inheriting God's promises. It is impossible to please God without faith. *And without faith it is impossible to please God, because anyone who comes to him must believe that he exists and that he rewards those who earnestly seek him* (Hebrews 11:6).

> **Revival Tip:** *It is impossible to please God without faith.*

Renewing Your Mind

Living an active life in God's economy requires a constant renewing of your mind against what the world is telling you. *Do not conform any longer to the pattern of this world, but be transformed by the renewing of your mind. Then you will be able to test and approve what God's will is—His good, pleasing and perfect will* (Romans 12:2). It is clear here that God's will is always good for you, pleasing, and perfect. But often bad circumstances and listening to what the media or well-meaning people say will have you thinking God's will is to make you stay poor, suffer, and be punished for your sins even though you know in your head that you are forgiven. You must continually renew your mind to what God initially promised you—what His will is—and believe Him.

> **Revival Tip:** *Staying in God's word is the best way to keep your mind renewed.*

So how do you keep your mind renewed? John 8:31–32 says, *If you hold to my teaching, you are really my disciples. ³²Then you will know the truth, and the truth will set you free.* Staying in God's word is probably the best way to renew your mind. In my house, we have posted verses on the bathroom mirror, in the office, and other places we frequent. By consistently reading those verses, we go beyond memorizing them, and bury them deep within ourselves (see Deuteronomy 6:4–9). By doing this, we stop simply "knowing" what God says, and begin to *know* in our hearts what is true.

Additionally, you must learn to put into action 1 Peter 5:7. *Cast all your anxiety on him because he cares for you.* Philippians 4:6–7 says, *Do not be anxious about anything, but in everything, by prayer and petition, with thanksgiving, present your requests to God. ⁷And the peace of God, which transcends all understanding, will guard your hearts and your minds in Christ Jesus.* In this world, anxiety runs rampant. Otherwise there wouldn't be so many verses about how to defeat anxiety in the Bible, or so many drugs to treat anxiety and depression being advertised on television.

Many people asked us how we knew the new job we were believing for was in God's will. It took some time, but we came to realize that God intends for us to live in His Kingdom, which includes living with His blessings, joy, and expectation of great things, even in our lives here on earth.

The bottom line of what we learned was that if you have peace and joy about a promise or what you are believing for, even when you don't know where your next meal is coming from or see the manifestation of the promise, that peace and joy is a sign that you are acting in accordance with God's will. If you do get that peace, despite what you see, you will know you are in God's will and your mind will be renewed once again to His promise. However, if you are anxious or fearful about it, even after praying about it, you may need to reevaluate what you are believing Him to provide. *Let the peace of Christ rule in your hearts, since as members of one body you were called to peace. And be thankful* (Colossians 3:15).

"Then Abram gave him a tenth of everything."

Genesis 14:20

Chapter 10

The Tithe

"Tithe" means "one tenth." The principle of tithing is first mentioned in Genesis 4:3–5. *In the course of time Cain brought some of the fruits of the soil as an offering to the Lord. ⁴But Abel brought fat portions from some of the firstborn of his flock. The Lord looked with favor on Abel and his offering, ⁵but on Cain and his offering he did not look with favor.* The principle of giving the first portion—the best portion—to God in thanksgiving for all He has provided is first mentioned with Abel.

Cain did bring an offering, but he kept the best for himself (Hebrews 11:4). Therefore God honored Abel and blessed the labor of his hands, but Cain became angry because he did not receive the same blessing. God knows that when you honor Him first, it releases His hand to work miracles with the remaining 90% (see *Authority*, Chapter 6).

Law vs. Principle

Some people think that we don't have to tithe anymore because it was an Old Testament law, which we as Christians are not bound to obey. However, before God gave the Israelites the Law, Abram recognized the principle of tithing when he met with the high priest Melchizedek. Genesis 14:20 says, *Then Abram gave him a tenth of everything.* Tithing is a principle first.

> **Revival Tip**
>
> *Tithing is a principle that was established long before the Law.*

God created the world with the principle of gravity in place so we wouldn't all float away into space. This principle still applies to our daily lives whether we consciously recognize it or not. Therefore, even though we are under the New Covenant that God made through Jesus, the Kingdom principle of honoring God with your firstfruits, like the principle of gravity, remains. Under the New Covenant, tithing is not required in order to be saved. In addition, acts of animal sacrifice to cover our sins, and other laws of the Old Testament are not necessary to be saved today. However, we still abide by the wisdom in Proverbs and the Ten Commandments, for instance, because the Holy Spirit inspires us to do so.

This is why we tithe. We don't tithe to get God to bless us or because we're cursed if we don't. Many well-meaning people, quoting Malachi 3:9, teach that we are cursed if we don't tithe. However, the curse God is talking about in this verse is the curse of the Law, from which Christ has redeemed us (Galatians 3:13). While we're not cursed if we don't tithe, there are consequences if we choose not to, because our closed hearts can keep us from experiencing the fullness of God's blessing in our lives.

God has already blessed us with everything we need through Jesus. Tithing is an expression of our love, gratitude, and honor for God, and our trust and faith in Him. Giving and trusting God with our money allows the blessings God already has for us to flow into our lives. If you want more in-depth teaching on this subject, check out Andrew Womack's free audio teaching, *Financial Stewardship*, at www.awmi.net.

Don't feel like you must *pay* tithe. The principle of tithing exists to honor the Lord and His command, not as another bill to pay. God has always valued relationship first. He wants us to love Him completely, not to feel a religious obligation to Him or any other ministry. Religious acts with no relationship can kill your spirit, but relationship is the source of life. God wants you to honor Him based on your relationship with Him, not because you have some religious duty to fulfill.

> *Revival Tip*
>
> **We don't tithe to get God to bless us or because we're cursed if we don't.**

Religious tradition might bring comfort, but it will not sustain you through the most difficult trials you are sure to face. If you view tithe as a bill or obligation, you are not giving freely as a choice because of your relationship with God. He has given you free will for a reason. He prefers it when we choose to honor and love Him. *Each man should give what he has decided in his heart to give, not reluctantly or **under compulsion**, for God loves a cheerful giver* (2 Corinthians 9:7, emphasis added). There is great reward in giving because you *want* to.

> **Revival Tip**
>
> *Religious tradition might bring comfort, but it won't sustain you.*

We can't love God with our whole hearts without tithing. But we can tithe without loving God with our whole hearts. God wants both. Let me explain. Yes, you can love God, but you are not totally trusting him with everything you have—including your money—unless you tithe. By giving away that first 10% and enabling Him to work with the other 90%, you are putting your faith and trust in Him to provide for what that other 10% could have been spent on. However, you can tithe out of obligation, out of religious duty, and not truly love or trust Him.

Since tithing is not an obligation, if we mess up, it's OK. We're already forgiven. For instance, some people have asked if they should offer a back-tithe for when they were not tithing in the past. Personally, I believe if God is asking you to sow a specific amount and you have a peace about it, you should do it. However, if you decide to start now, God does not expect you to "catch up" on tithe for your income over your entire pre-tithing life. That is unreasonable! But from now on, try to make every effort to tap into the principle of tithing.

If this principle wasn't important, it would have been done away with when Jesus came, and we would cease to see any benefit to our lives. Today and forever, the principle of tithing exists for *our* benefit, not God's, so whenever you decide to start, it will begin to produce fruit in your life.

The Power of "Each One"

When we hold onto our tithe, we are holding the church back from fully functioning as God designed. If every person in the church were tithing, there would be enough overflow for the creation and functioning of schools, community outreaches, medical facilities, food banks, etc. But because many people do not understand the principle of tithing, the church cannot do all the things it is called to do and unfortunately the government has stepped in and gained control of many of these activities instead, which can further hurt the community through higher taxes, by removing incentives for personal responsibility, etc.

> **Revival Tip:** *If every churchgoer tithes, miracles will happen.*

Likewise, if everyone is tithing, the burden is lifted from a few, and miracles can happen. For instance, my pastor recently demonstrated the ability of each member of the church to impact a life. Without telling us what he was doing, he asked every single person in the room to put only $1—no more than that—in the offering buckets. His point was to show that when each of us gives a little, a lot of good can come of it and it doesn't hurt us individually at all.

> **Revival Tip**
>
> *When each one gives a little, a lot of good comes of it and it doesn't hurt.*

The total amount collected was $300, and our pastor in turn gave the money to a single mom in the church who had lost her job and was being evicted from her apartment. We had no idea of her need, but that $300 that was initially collected turned into over $1,000 by the end of the day, and it met a large portion of her need. She had been honoring God with her tithe on every bit of income she could scrape together, and a miracle was provided to her. If you are concerned with letting go of that 10%, be encouraged by her story. If you give God the first 10%, He will show you how to do more with 90% than the 100% you initially had.

Another story of the power of "each one" occurred in our church a couple years ago. A local food bank and housing rehabilitation ministry in town had lost their government funding for their housing program. The amount they normally received annually was $30,000. Our church of 500 people came together and raised an offering to cover that program's expenses. We raised a total of $40,000 in that one offering and our pastor was able to deliver a check to them the very next morning. We are still hearing the stories of those who work with the ministry and how that single act is still impacting lives. By the church coming together and doing what it was designed to do, thousands of lives were changed!

Some people have said that we must have some "rich" people in our church. Many churches probably have a couple of affluent families, but I was in the service that day and saw the number of people contributing to this ministry's need. After the count was in, it was determined that we had 99% participation. Even college students gave something. As little as $5 was contributed, but God multiplied it all together and a miracle took place.

Not only were we able to meet a major need in our community, but they had $10,000 extra to sustain their programs and help even more local jobless and homeless families. If only 50% of the people participated, this need would not have been met. This is the power of "each one" coming together out of a love for God and His desire to reach the world through our giving. Imagine what would happen if every single church member tithed on a regular basis! Imagine what a difference that would make to *your* community!

10% of Gross, Net, Time, or What?

When you get your paycheck, how do you calculate your tithe? Do you tithe on the amount after taxes, insurance, and other withholdings are taken out? The going consensus of Christian financial experts like Crown Financial Ministries®, Dave Ramsey, and Gary Keese are that we should be tithing on our gross income. Personally,

I have gone from tithing on the net amount (after taxes, etc.) to tithing on the gross (the number at the top of your paycheck), so I can attest to the fact that their advice is correct.

Here is my reasoning why. When you tithe on the lowest number on your paycheck—what's deposited into your bank account—you are actually giving your "firstfruit" to someone other than God. The government takes taxes out of the gross amount of what you make. By allowing them to have the top position on your paycheck, you are not entrusting God with the first and the best. I challenge you to entrust God with 10% of the gross amount on your paycheck and see what happens!

> **Revival Tip:** *I challenge you to entrust God with 10% of gross and see what happens!*

For those who own their own business, like me, you might think you should also tithe on the gross of your paycheck. However, most small business owners don't get much of a "paycheck," if any, and what about the business itself? Should the business tithe? I believe if you are a business owner and want to entrust your business to God's authority, your business should be tithing. In general, the recommendation is that a business should tithe after its basic expenses—employee payroll and those expenses necessary to keep the business in operation—are met. Since tithe is on the "increase" (see Deuteronomy 14:22). For a business, that would be its profit.

Chapter 10: The Tithe

Business owners typically must plan their budgets months in advance. They must be sure the basic expenses of the business are paid and there is enough seed for future growth. Then the profit is determined. A good example of this is the nation of Israel—a mostly agricultural society. If a farmer gave his seed (what was necessary to produce his next crop) to a priest, he would not have seed to plant for the next year's harvest. Seed was typically not given except in the case of grain at particular feasts, but that was given as an offering, not as the tithe. The tithe was on the "firstfruits" of their harvest. After everything comes in and we pay the bills that are essential for keeping the business healthy and going, we tithe.

In the case of my business, we tithe after our necessary costs of goods sold are met. That is, what comes in minus the payroll and direct expenses incurred for client projects. Then we give God 10% before we pay the rest of our expenses (Internet, phone, rent, utilities, etc.). We know we are actually giving a little more than the normal tithe, but we also understand the importance of sowing additional seed for our business's growth.

> *Revival* Tip — **The tithe should be on the "firstfruits" of your harvest, not your seed.**

Though we use the measure of 10% to determine what we will give each month, and it is before some of our normal operating expenses, we count a portion of that measure as an offering—a seed—that we are planting in faith that God will open doors for our business to grow and give us the ability to bless others even more. We will go more in-depth on why we choose to do this in the next two chapters.

> **Revival Tip:** *When we had no income, we tithed of our time.*

I have heard of people who do not have an income give of their time instead. Indeed, when my husband and I had no income, we both volunteered time at our church. However, we still tithed on every bit of income that came in, no matter how small. You may not have a job, but you may have someone buy something from you, like baked goods or furniture. We sold a lot of our belongings to make ends meet, and every time we tithed 10% off the top of what we gained. After all, there was barely enough to cover a bill, so why not act with a little faith and trust that God would stretch that tiny amount to cover all our needs? And He did.

In some countries, you get a tax break for giving to a nonprofit. Though this is nice, it should not be a requirement for you to have met before you tithe. Tithing is a Biblical principle, not governed by man's laws. If you want to put your name on it so that you get that tax break, go ahead. We do. By saving money on our taxes, we are able to sow more into God's kingdom. And in our experience, God has been a lot more responsible with our money than any government established by man.

In the next chapter, we will discuss offerings, or giving in addition to the tithe. Tithing is the Kingdom principle for establishing complete trust of your financial life to God. Offerings further increase access to God's provision and allow Him to work more miracles in your financial world.

"...men will praise God for ... your generosity in sharing with them and with everyone else."

2 Corinthians 9:13

Chapter 11

The Offering

Interestingly enough, Jesus didn't teach most about tithing, but about giving. Giving allows us to be a blessing to others. This is one reason why Jesus said it is truly *more blessed to give than to receive* (Acts 20:35). Offerings are to be given in addition to your tithe. Offerings, when sown into fertile ground, will reap an even larger harvest than tithing can do alone. 2 Corinthians 9:13 says, *Because of the service by which you have proved yourselves, men will praise God for the obedience that accompanies your confession of the gospel of Christ, and for your generosity in sharing with them and with everyone else.*

Your act of cheerful giving will cause others to glorify God. We are blessed to be a blessing! And by blessing others, it leads them back to their Creator. What better witness could you have than a sacrifice you make that guides other people to know the Lord? Just as "actions speak louder than words," the gift of a large tip and the simple message that God loves them will speak more to a waitress than a gospel tract left with a minimal tip on the table. Generosity in your giving (both financially and of your time) changes lives, not preaching at people.

The Vacuum for Possibility

Giving in addition to the tithe also creates a space in your finances only God can fill, which He will fill to overflowing so that you can be an even bigger blessing. In Philippians 4:10–20, Paul speaks to the church that sent him provisions for his ministry. They obviously had a need, but they gave anyway. In verse 19 is the famous text, *And my God will meet all your needs according to his glorious riches in Christ Jesus.* The people of this church were clearly participating in offerings—giving to a ministry that was not directly related to their church—and all their needs were met because of their act of giving.

> **Revival Tip:** *When God fills a space you create, He fills it to overflowing.*

Obedience in giving creates a vacuum for God's provision. When you give more money away, that money can be used to get something you or your family may want. However, by giving it away as an offering and placing your trust in God, you are giving Him another opportunity to show up and create a miracle. Giving of offerings requires a step (sometimes leap) of faith. Sometimes it may feel like it takes a larger amount of faith than tithing, but it sets the stage for an increase of provision in your life.

When you give offerings, your life will not be dictated by circumstances. Possibility is found in the place of prayer and stepping out above and beyond what you can do yourself. It is purchased in our obedience to give—beyond the tithe. When you give, God gives you more so that you can give even more. It is a continuous cycle designed to use you to meet the needs of others, turning them to the truth of their Creator who loves them, and directing the course of your financial future.

> **Revival Tip:** *Possibility is found in stepping out beyond what you can do alone.*

Now he who supplies seed to the sower and bread for food will also supply and increase your store of seed and will enlarge the harvest of your righteousness (2 Corinthians 9:10). Do you have seed you can sow? Some increase as a result of your obedience with tithe? Use it as offering. Plant it and it will bring a harvest more bountiful than the amount of seed you had before. Step toward the possibility in your future.

Sowing and Reaping

Luke 8:4–8 tells the Parable of the Sower. *While a large crowd was gathering and people were coming to Jesus from town after town, he told this parable:* ⁵*"A farmer went out to sow his seed. As he was scattering the seed, some fell along the path; it was trampled on, and the birds of the air ate it up.* ⁶*Some fell on rock, and when it came up, the plants withered because they had no moisture.* ⁷*Other seed fell among thorns, which grew up with it and choked the plants.* ⁸*Still other seed fell on good soil.*

It came up and yielded a crop, a hundred times more than was sown." An obvious point of this story is that where you sow is important. But if that is all you see, you are missing another major point.

> **Revival Tip:** **Sow your tithe and offerings intentionally into fertile soil.**

First of all, the farmer had an intention to sow a specific type of seed and expected at least some of it to return a harvest. Sow your tithe and offerings intentionally into fertile soil. Remember that you are not giving to a man's ministry, or an organization. You are giving first and foremost to the purposes of God through your local church.

Even if you discover that a church or an authority in the church is misusing funds, you need to remember that you have sown into God's Kingdom, not that particular ministry. Yes, your funds may have been used for something you do not agree with, and yes, they could even have been stolen by someone who lacks moral character. But as soon as you find out, the responsible thing to do is to start finding more fertile ground in which to sow. Ask God to direct you. You should not be so focused on what your funds are used for, or so afraid to sow because of someone misusing it, that you avoid the principle altogether. He will always provide for those who honor Him. If you are honoring Him with your tithe, He will protect you.

As humans, we tend to give our money only to things that make us feel good. If the pastor is preaching something we like, we may feel like giving more. If he teaches something that doesn't feel good to us, especially if it is the truth and we feel uncomfortable, we may resist tithing and giving. There is always going to be resistance to your spiritual growth. But without resistance, there is no growth.

Think of when a planted seed sprouts. The newly formed, weak little sprout has to push its way out of the hard casing of the seed. The very act of pushing through that shell—resistance—strengthens the plant so that when it grows above the ground, it grows strong. If you sow with the right motive in your heart—to honor God—and retain His promise in His word that He has plans to prosper you and not harm you (Jeremiah 29:11), you will find your life becoming stronger to the point that when the storm hits, the branches of your life stand firm against the raging winds of circumstances.

> *Revival Tip:* **Resistance strengthens us to grow strong.**

When you choose to give, ask God where He would have you give. You may have an opportunity to sow into a ministry or a project at your church such as a building fund, or there may be a ministry outside your church that has touched your life in some way and you want to help them touch others. For instance, my family gives offerings to our church in addition to our tithe, but we also choose to give to other ministries that have been a blessing to us. By giving to these ministries, it has enabled them to reach many others with the message of God's love. It has also blessed us to be obedient to what God has asked us to do.

> **Revival Tip:** *A farmer does not sow beans and expect wheat.*

Another overlooked part of the parable is the fact that farmers usually sow a specific type of seed and expect a harvest of that plant. They do not sow bean seeds expecting wheat. Or soy and expect corn. In the parable, Jesus is specifically talking about God's Word being sown for the lost to hear and be saved (Luke 8:11). In our lives of honoring His Word and commands, we should sow seed expecting a specific harvest.

I am not talking about sowing your finances and expecting God to drop one million dollars in your lap. But I am talking about sowing in expectation of a future harvest of a specific promise from God—one that may not happen right away. Some seeds take longer to germinate than others. And you still have to do your part to care for that young plant before you can reap a harvest from it. You still have to take steps of faith as God leads you toward your harvest.

For instance, when my husband was looking for a job, we sat down and made a specific list of what we wanted in that job. We prayed over it several times a day, and wrote on our tithe and offerings that we were believing and sowing for it. On that list was a specific income level, location, climate, and amenities of the workplace. I thought several items on the list were impossible, which of course was no problem to God. Today, we are moved to the location we prayed for and my husband has a job that fulfills every single item on our list—no matter that some of them were "impossible."

For instance, we wanted to move somewhere that had 200 frost-free days per year. This limited the geography considerably. My husband also wanted a walking trail in a park to be one minute from where he worked. Having worked in corporate America, I thought this one was impossible! However, not only are we now living in a city that gets exactly 200 frost-free days per year, but there are walking trails and a small park in the office park where he works. And you can bet my husband timed his walk to the trails on his first day—60 seconds from his building to the park. That convinced me that God does care about the desires of our hearts and will honor our obedience regarding the principle of sowing a specific seed.

> **Revival Tip:** *God dwells in the "impossible."*

This job was not something selfish we were asking God to provide. It was something that was promised. God promised to supply all our needs. And all our needs were not previously being met. Some people don't agree with sowing intentionally, but having learned the reasoning behind it, I encourage you to try it. If you know God's promises, and you sow and believe for something so specific you do not think you can find it on your own, it is a chance for God to show up. And when that thing happens, especially if it has impossibilities in it, God has to be the one to get the credit.

> **Revival Tip:** God wants to be the one to get the credit.

Do you see why He loves it when we are specific and intentional in our belief? Because otherwise, if all we said was we wanted a new job, we could have taken the credit for finding that job all on our own. But by believing, sowing, and being specific, we have no choice but to give God the credit when we share the story. And we have done this with other things, too, including housing, cars, and income levels of our business. Every time, God has shown up and provided exactly what we asked, giving us more incredible stories to share to encourage others who are struggling in their belief.

Legalism vs. Faith

It is possible to give offerings and not experience God's abundant blessing and provision, especially if we are giving out of a "debt" we feel we owe to God. Jesus came and paid that debt in full. We are so blessed to be able to live under the New Covenant! No longer do we need to abide by the old laws in order to be forgiven and have God's hand on our lives, including our finances. But we do need to have faith to experience everything He has for us. Even if you cannot sow very much, sow something. Give something. When my husband and I were searching for his job, we decided to give above our tithes, just $5 a week. We weren't even buying our own groceries at the time!

Some people thought we were throwing our money away. But we chose two ministries that had helped us grow spiritually and gave $10 to each every month. Now we are supporting those ministries and several more at $25 a month each and able to sow into special projects through our church. That little seed we started planting has grown to the point we can give even more without first checking our bank account balance. It is a sense of financial freedom we had never experienced before. I get a thrill every time I get to give! God honored our faith as cheerful givers, not because we felt we had to do it to "get" something from Him, but because we believed He had already promised it to us and wanted to unlock whatever was hindering it from being manifest in our lives.

> *Revival Tip:* ***It's the act of faith, not the dollar amount that matters.***

It is the act of faith, not the dollar amount that matters. *But a poor widow came and put in two very small copper coins,* worth only a fraction of a penny. ⁴³Calling his disciples to him, Jesus said, "I tell you the truth, this poor widow has put more into the treasury than all the others. ⁴⁴They all gave out of their wealth; but she, out of her poverty, put in everything—all she had to live on" (Mark 12:42–44).

God does not call everyone to give up all their belongings and wipe their bank accounts clean to give to Him. However, this poor widow only had enough for a seed. She gave with a huge act of faith that her meager seed would produce a harvest. Others who were "giving out of their abundance" were not sacrificing as she did.

Even when your harvest begins to come, I challenge you to continue giving enough that it creates a vacuum only God can fill, even if it seems impossible. Allow God to build your faith in Him and come through with provision in such a way that you could never get there on your own. And then give Him the glory so that others may see your testimony and grow in their relationship with their Creator!

"Death and life are in the power of the tongue."

Proverbs 18:21, NKJV

Chapter 12

Declaration

This final chapter confronts one of the most important reasons people do not see their harvests or the fruits of what they sow through tithes and offerings.

Realizing the Power of Your Words

God's Word, the Bible, is the foundation of your faith. Deuteronomy 30:14 says, *...the word is very near you; it is in your mouth and in your heart so you may obey it.* We have seen how God does not want His children living in poverty. You must speak it ("in your mouth"), believe it ("in your heart"), obey it, and then watch Him provide so that you can do what He asks.

Your words have the power to keep the financial blessing from being provided to you by God. *From the fruit of his mouth a man's stomach is filled; with the harvest from his lips he is satisfied* (Proverbs 18:20). What do you speak? Speech is most used today for simple communication. But the power of the tongue is evident with the creation of the universe. *And God said...and there was* (Genesis 1:3). God did not create the earth, stars, and heavens by molding some clay or primordial soup. He spoke. By creating us in His image, He gave us the power to create with our words.

> **Revival Tip:** *God gave us the power to create with our words.*

You have probably heard the childhood rhyme, "sticks and stones may break my bones, but words will never hurt me." But you know that to be a blatant lie. How many times were you hurt by someone putting you down? Saying you're worthless? How often have words hurt you—or built you up? Why do you think there is such a focus in parenting books on what parents say to their kids? How many counselors and psychiatrists would be out of work if people stopped demeaning others with their words? *Death and life are in the power of the tongue* (Proverbs 18:21, NKJV).

I have seen many lives ripped apart by something someone said. Whether you personally believe it or not, the power to curse or bless is in your tongue. I was blessed to have parents who continually built me up with their speech. However, many of my friends still struggle with feelings of inadequacy because they were brought up in homes with parents who abused their God-given power and spoke death and curses over their lives. They were told things like, "You will never amount to anything" or, "You can't do anything right." Unfortunately for my friends who have gone through this day after day in their childhood, the fight to continually feel worth something is still an uphill battle. We should all learn this lesson: you form your future and others' futures by what you say.

Speaking in Faith

In the same way as with people, your financial situation is affected by your words. The more bad things you say about it, the worse it gets. Once you start saying, "I'm broke, I'll never have enough," you have opened the door for Satan to attack your finances. Or even worse, you have shut the door on God's ability to bless your finances. It doesn't matter if you are tithing and giving or not. You are cursing the very gift—the seed—before it can grow. You are not watering the seed God has blessed you with.

> **Revival Tip:** *Be careful not to curse the seed before it can grow.*

Speaking about your circumstances reinforces them positively or negatively. There was a point in time when my husband and I went through the trial of having no income that we spoke over and over, "We have no money, God isn't providing," etc., etc. As soon as we started speaking the opposite—"We have provision, God *is* providing"—and training ourselves to speak out loud these words when those negative thoughts struck, something changed inside. We moved from cursing the blessing God wanted to give us to *being* blessed.

It is a mindset we had to change. Although our circumstances didn't change immediately, by shifting that mindset and speaking things that weren't as though they were out loud (Romans 4:17), there was peace inside us. We had already been believing for our circumstances to change, but not speaking—confessing—the changes we wanted to see out loud. Romans 10:9 says, ...*if you confess with your mouth, "Jesus is Lord," and believe in your heart that God raised him from the dead, you will be saved*. You must do both. You must believe and confess—speak it out loud—to be saved from your circumstances, your financial situation, and ultimately saved from the curse of this fallen world. My pastor once saw a bumper sticker that read, "God said it. I believe it. And that settles it." But he changed this saying to, "God said it. I believe it. I *declare* it. And *that* settles it." You must believe *and* say it—not just believe.

God has done His part. He has already promised you provision—more than enough. You need to do your part. It is time for you to speak the promise and thank God for it, even if you can't see it. Ask God what He is saying and declare that. There is something about speaking it out loud that combats your negative thoughts and further strengthens your faith.

> **𝑅𝑒𝑣𝑖𝑣𝑎𝑙 Tip:** *Speaking out loud combats negativity and strengthens your faith.*

When you start speaking and declaring, it is difficult. Not only do you see the hopeless circumstances every

Chapter 12: Declaration

day, but you may feel all alone and even a bit silly. It is important to surround yourself with people who can speak positively into your world. If you have friends who continually put you down, even jokingly, it is time to ask God to provide you some new friends. If you have friends who are constantly speaking negatively over their own lives, you need to put some distance between you and them so that you aren't tempted to follow suit.

> *Revival* Tip — **Surround yourself with others who continually build you up.**

There is something to be said for reaching out to them, but you need to be in a position to help them and you cannot if you are putting yourself down, too. If you ask God for friends who can help build you up, or a church family who understands declaring and the power of speech, He will provide. And as you surround yourself with others who continually build you up, you will find the strength to begin declaring blessing over your financial life as well.

Confessing in Prayer

Prayer is vital for connection with God and others. It strengthens you in faith by conversing with God and allowing Him to speak to you. Praying with others also builds your relationship with them by allowing you to see into their hearts and be supported in your time of need.

Prayer does not have to happen in a dark closet where you go for 30 minutes each day to talk with God. Prayer is actually just a conversation with God. It can be a set amount of time each day or a continuous conversation throughout the day. I find that by keeping my heart open at all times and speaking to God throughout my day, I have a more lasting peace and can better handle unexpected stresses that arise. And when something comes up and I say, "But God, *you* said...," it reminds me of His promise, and also continues the fight out loud for what He has rightfully given me.

> **Revival Tip:** *Prayer is a simply a conversation with God.*

Labeling in Trust

As I talked about in Chapter 11 under *Sowing and Reaping,* labeling your gift is another way of declaring the promise God has given you. Labeling your tithe and offerings—writing on your check or envelope what you are believing for—is the difference between simple obedience and applied faith. It also enables others to support you in prayer when they see what you are believing for. What you believe for may be financial provision, the salvation of a loved one, emotional stability, a future mate, or strength in your marriage.

Chapter 12: Declaration

God's blessings may not be what you expect, but if they aren't, you can be assured they will be even better. Trust that He knows what you need—for you and others. *This is the confidence we have in approaching God: that if we ask anything according to his will, he hears us.* [15]*And if we know that he hears us—whatever we ask—we know that we have what we asked of him* (1 John 5:14–15).

God's will is to prosper us so that we can help others, not just help ourselves. So by having the proper heart posture, asking, believing, *and* confessing through our mouths or even the memo section of our checks, we will see His blessings come. These are some verses my husband and I keep close by our financial records and commit to our hearts often:

You do not have, because you do not ask God (James 4:2).

Therefore I tell you, whatever you ask for in prayer, believe that you have received it, and it will be yours (Mark 11:24).

Do not be anxious about anything, but in everything, by prayer and petition, with thanksgiving, present your requests to God (Philippians 4:6).

We live by faith, not by sight (2 Corinthians 5:7).

The bottom line is to not be anxious, to ask and declare, and to have the heart posture and understanding that you are not only asking for your needs to be met, but that you can meet the needs of others and give an amazing testimony to them of God's abundant provision. Now's your chance—go change the world. It's your turn for a *Financial Revival!*

"'Bring the whole tithe into the storehouse...Test me in this,' says the Lord Almighty, 'and see if I will not...pour out so much blessing that you will not have room enough for it.'"

Malachi 3:10

Appendix

Financially, what does it take a ministry to operate? This section features several ministries and charities and just some of the costs associated with keeping them running and fulfilling their God-given assignments. (Information taken from www.BBB.org.)

The American Red Cross

The Red Cross provides services to needy individuals through its various programs. The organization responds to about 70,000 disasters in the USA each year. They also provide education for responding to emergencies and process blood donations—more than 40% of the nation's blood supply.

Total operating costs and program expenses for Biomedical, Disaster, Health, International Relief, Community, and Armed Forces Services:

$333,106,667/month

To get involved and/or donate: www.redcross.org

The Bible League

The Bible League supplies Scriptures, Christian literature and training materials to churches and mission organizations around the world free of charge or at subsidized cost.

Total operating costs and program expenses for Bible and literature/training materials translation, creation, and distribution:

$3,300,833/month

To get involved and/or donate: www.BibleLeague.org

The Salvation Army

The Salvation Army works through a network of 8,500 facilities in communities throughout the U.S. They provide shelter for the homeless, gifts, groceries, missing persons services, day care, after-school activities and tutoring, job placement, Bible classes, summer camps, and disaster relief.

Total operating costs and program expenses for education and publications, training, development, and disaster services:

$7,653,071/month

To get involved and/or donate: www.salvationarmyusa.org

Answers in Genesis

Answers in Genesis provides teaching seminars, a radio program, educational materials, the Creation Museum, and other programs designed to enable Christians to defend their faith and proclaim the gospel of Jesus Christ effectively.

Total operating costs and program expenses for training programs, operating costs, and educational materials:

$1,711,823/month

To get involved and/or donate: www.AnswersInGenesis.org

A Local Church

The local church provides the support structure and training necessary to grow in the Christian walk.

Operating costs for an 80,000 sq ft building including *only* rent, utilities, and staff salaries:

$64,000/month

To get involved: Sow into your local church!

Revival Tip | Remember the **power** of *"each one!"*

"And you will be called priests of the Lord, you will be named ministers of our God."

Isaiah 61:6

About the Author

Kristen Eckstein is an author, graphic designer, and writing and publishing coach. Raised in full-time ministry as a pastor's kid, she learned the principles explained in this book at an early age. She has participated in multiple missions trips and taught in various churches, however, until recently she never considered herself to be "in ministry."

She now realizes that her ministry is to her clients and readers. Using the gifts God has blessed her with to operate the business she and her husband started in 2004, together they reach out to as many lives as they can with the hope God has given them. Kristen has learned that though she is unable to change every life herself, she can enable other ministries to do what they are called to through ongoing financial support.

In her "free time" she reads some of her favorite Christian thriller authors and enjoys quiet time with her family. Learn more about Kristen at www.KristenEckstein.com.

Other Books by Kristen

Is your checkbook on life support?

This book will show you how to:
- Survive on very little income.
- Pay down your debt for good.
- Not have to struggle financially.
- Have enough money for your normal bills and debt payments.
- Stretch your money farter than you thought it would go.
- Find the things you need cheap or free.

ISBN: 978-0976791355

$9.95 *Available at all fine retailers.*

It's like MySpace for Kids and Teens!

These books are address books made especially for kids and teens. Keep track of over 45 of your family members and friends by having them fill out their own "All About Me" and "My Favorites" pages.

You and your friends are sure to have a ton of fun with this book!

Note: These books contains "religious" references.

Kids ISBN: 978-0976131700

Teens ISBN: 978-0976131717

$8.95 each *Available at all fine retailers.*

www.ingramcontent.com/pod-product-compliance
Lightning Source LLC
LaVergne TN
LVHW021716060526
838200LV00050B/2688